ESL

ADDISON-WESLEY

Michael Walker

Original Music by Bob Schneider

Addison-Wesley Publishing Company

Reading, Massachusetts • Menlo Park, California • New York • Don Mills, Ontario • Wokingham, England
Amsterdam • Bonn • Sydney • Singapore • Tokyo • Madrid • San Juan

A Publication of the World Language Division

Editor-in-Chief: Judith Bittinger

Project Director: Elinor Chamas

Editorial Development: Claire Smith, Talbot Hamlin

Production/Manufacturing: James W. Gibbons

Rights Coordination: Merle Sciacca

Design, Art Direction, and Production: Taurins Design Associates, New York

Cover Art: Elizabeth Miles

Illustrators: Teresa Anderko 46, 47, 76, 118; Donna Ayers 120, 121; Natalie Babbitt 80, 81, 82, 83, 84, 85; Don Baker 8, 28, 48, 66, 68, 73, 94, 95; Doron Ben-Ami 34, 35, 54, 96; Lee Lee Brazeal 99, 119; Denise Brunkus 4, 5, 24, 25, 44, 45, 64, 65, 86, 87, 106, 107; Chi Chung 20, 21, 22, 23, 69; Ray Cruz 122, 123, 124, 125, 126, 127; Mena Dolobowsky 16, 36, 56, 98, 110; Eldon Doty 37; David Frampton 38, 39, 78, 79; Simon Galkin 100; Diane Teske Harris 29, 57, 90, 91, 111; Meryl Henderson 6, 26, 88, 108; Amy Hill 17; Karen Loccisano 12, 13, 49, 52, 53, 72; Elizabeth Miles 40, 41, 42, 43; Brenda Mishell (handwriting) 15, 35, 55, 75, 97, 117; Cyd Moore 9, 77, 114, 115; Vo-Dinh Mai 102, 103, 104, 105; Deborah Pinkney 7, 27, 67, 75, 89, 109; Roger Roth 32, 33; David Tamura 60, 61, 62, 63

Photographers: Allied Artists, Bad Men of Tombstone 95; A.W. Ambler, Photo Researchers, National Audubon Society 19; Area Research Center, Murphy Library 14; AT & T Bell Laboratories 30; Bettman Archive left 10, top left, top right, bottom 11, middle left 31, top, bottom 51; M. Brady, N.Y. Historical Society 50; Kathleen Sands Boehmer 97; Robert Caputo, Photo Researchers 59; Alan Carey, The Image Works middle left 93; Culver Pictures right 10; Ellis Herwig, Stock Boston top 93; George Laycock, Photo Researchers bottom right 93; Tom McHugh, Photo Researchers 18, Steinhart Aquarium right 71, 101; Loren McIntyre bottom right 112, 113; N.Y. Public Library top left 71; N.Y. Zoological Society 58; Parker Bros. bottom right 31; H. Rogers, Monkmeyer 74; Leonard Lee Rue, Photo Researchers 92; Smithsonian Institution top left #A42103, bottom right 70 #A5052; Thomas Alva Edison Foundation top left 31; Van Nostrand Photos, Photo Researchers 116

Acknowledgments: Page 37, "The Meal," from *Dogs and Dragons, Trees and Dreams*, by Karla Kuskin. Copyright © 1962 by Karla Kuskin. Reprinted by permission of Harper & Row, Publishers, Inc. Pages 80-85, "The Something," Adaptation of *The Something*, by Natalie Babbitt. Copyright © 1970 by Natalie Babbitt. Reprinted by permission of Farrar, Straus and Giroux, Inc. Pages 102-105, Adapted selection from *The Land I Lost*, by Huynh Quang Nhuong. Copyright © 1982 by Huynh Quang Nhuong. Reprinted by permission of Harper & Row, Publishers, Inc. Page 119, "Ears Hear," by Lucia and James Hymes, Jr., from *Oodles of Noodles*, © 1964, Addison-Wesley Publishing Company, Inc., Reading Massachusetts. Poem. Reprinted with permission. Pages 122-127, Alexander and the Terrible, Horrible, No Good, Very Bad Day, reprinted by permission of Macmillan Publishing Company. Text copyright © 1972 by Judith Viorst. Pictures copyright © 1972 by Ray Cruz. Copyright © 1974 by Judith Viorst.

ISBN 0-201-57819-0

4 5 6 7 8 9 10 11 12-DA-96 95 94 93 92

Contents

Unit 1 Featuring LIFE SKILLS: Role-playing greetings, polite inquiries ♦ STUDY SKILLS: Skimming for information about transportation; research and report ♦ FABLE: "The Boy Who Cried Wolf" ♦ PLAY: "Rabbit and Tiger" (Hispanic tale)   **4**

Unit 2 Featuring LIFE SKILLS: Role-playing purchasing food ♦ STUDY SKILLS: Skimming for information about inventions/inventors; research and report ♦ POEM: "The Meal" by Karla Kuskin ♦ CLASSIC FICTION: "Through the Looking Glass" from the book by Lewis Carroll   **24**

Unit 3 Featuring LIFE SKILLS: Role-playing asking for and giving directions; map-reading ♦ STUDY SKILLS: Skimming for information about famous people; research and report ♦ FABLE: "The Lion and the Mouse" ♦ BIOGRAPHY: "George Washington Carver"   **44**

Unit 4 Featuring LIFE SKILLS: Role-playing using the telephone ♦ STUDY SKILLS: Skimming for information about famous events; research and report ♦ POEM: "Bed in Summer" by Robert Louis Stevenson ♦ CONTEMPORARY FICTION: "The Something" from the book by Natalie Babbitt   **64**

Unit 5 Featuring LIFE SKILLS: Role-playing making plans, buying tickets ♦ STUDY SKILLS: Skimming for information about life in the Arctic; research and report ♦ FABLE: "The Dog and the Bone ♦ AUTOBIOGRAPHY: "The Land I Lost" from the book by Hunyh Quang Nhuong   **86**

Unit 6 Featuring LIFE SKILLS: Role-playing buying clothes ♦ STUDY SKILLS: Skimming for information about life in the Amazon; research and report ♦ POEM: "Ears Hear" by Lucia and James L. Hymes, Jr. ♦ CONTEMPORARY FICTION: "Alexander and the Terrible, Horrible, No Good, Very Bad Day" from the book by Judith Viorst   **106**

Skills Index   **128**

Sunnyville is a medium-sized community. It's bigger than a village, but smaller than a city. Mrs. Martha Ruler is the mayor. She has a council to help her run Sunnyville. She and the council meet every week in the Sunnyville Town Hall.

Many people live and work in Sunnyville. They're proud of their community. Sunnyville is a clean, safe, and healthy place to live.

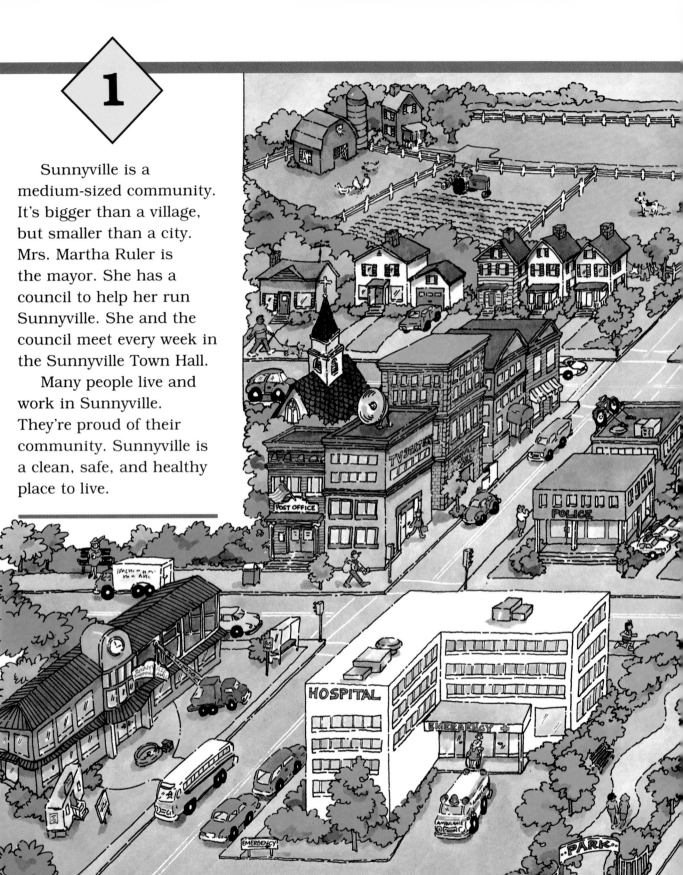

 Social studies: community life
Identifying/describing/counting
Asking for/giving information

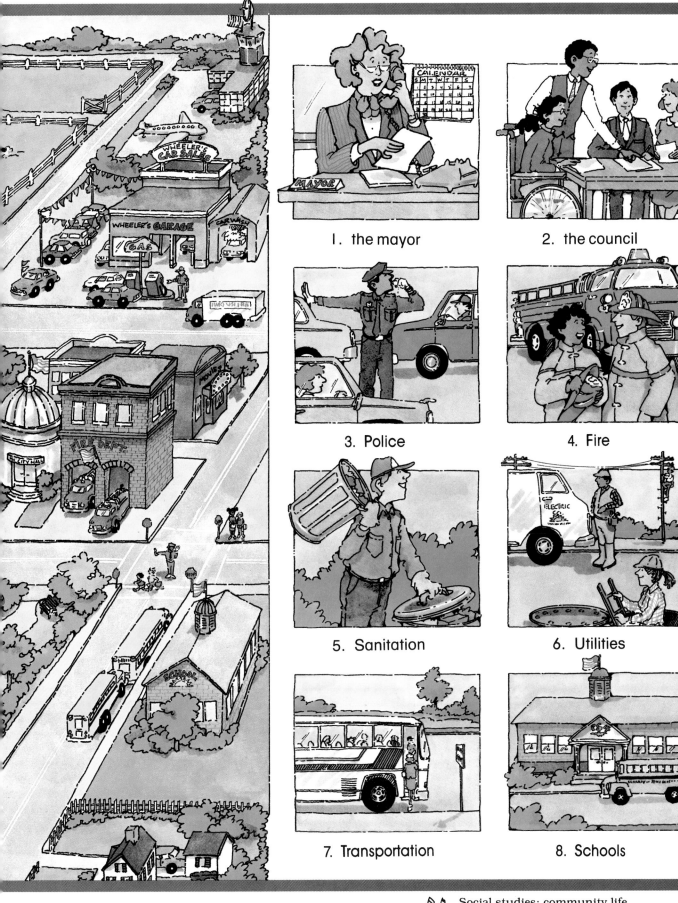

1. the mayor

2. the council

3. Police

4. Fire

5. Sanitation

6. Utilities

7. Transportation

8. Schools

Social studies: community life
Identifying/describing/counting
Asking for/giving information

5

DATA BANK

I feel great.	That's nice.	I'm not so good.	Sorry to hear that.
Wonderful.	I'm glad to hear it.	Awful.	That's too bad.
Terrific.	That's good.	Terrible.	Oh, I'm so sorry.

Greetings/polite exchanges
Role-playing fixed and free dialogues
Creating new dialogues from cues

Say the right thing!

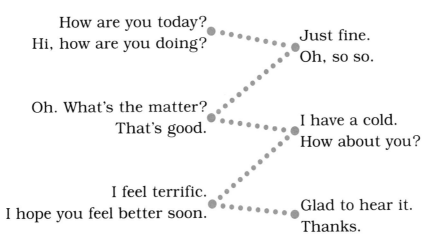

How are you today?
Hi, how are you doing? · · · · · Just fine.
· · Oh, so so.

Oh. What's the matter? · ·
That's good. · · · · I have a cold.
· · How about you?

I feel terrific.
I hope you feel better soon. · · · · · Glad to hear it.
Thanks.

Now make conversations with your partner.
Begin with these situations.

1. Your friend doesn't come to school. You call your friend to ask how he is.
   He has a cold.
   You say you hope he feels better soon.

2. You meet a friend at the store. She says hello and asks how you are.
   You say that you're fine and ask how she is.
   She feels wonderful.

Role-playing fixed dialogues
Understanding sequence in conversations
Creating new dialogues from cues

7

Pair Practice 1

I, we, you they		**He, she, it**	
walk	study	walks	studies
live	fix	lives	fixes
play		plays	

Take turns with your partner.
Ask and answer the questions.

A. 1. What do they buy? (bread)
   2. Where does he live? (Chicago)
   3. What does he like? (baseball)
   4. Where do you work? (store)

B. 1. What do they play? (football)
   2. What does she enjoy? (music)
   3. What do they say? (hello)
   4. What does he buy? (hat)

C. 1. What does he fix? (bikes)
   2. What do we brush? (teeth)
   3. What do you watch? (TV)
   4. What do you wash? (car)

D. 1. Where does the plane fly?
      (Miami)
   2. What do we study? (English)
   3. Where does she hurry to?
      (school)
   4. What do they carry?
      (bookbags)

Asking for/giving information (habitual actions)
Creating exchanges from cues
Spelling regular word endings

On weekends, my aunt Julie likes to drive to the mountains. She camps outdoors. Every Friday, she rushes home from work. She packs her things in a little trailer. She attaches the trailer to the back of her car. She drives up Route 93 to the mountains.

One weekend, Julie is on her way. She hears a police siren. She pulls off the highway to the side of the road. The police officer gets out of his car. Julie says, "What's wrong officer? Was I driving too fast?"

"Yes," replies the officer. "And you have two tail lights missing." Julie looks puzzled. She gets out of her car and walks to the back. She stops, throws her hands in the air, and screams! "Take it easy, lady," the officer says. "It's only a couple of tail lights."

"Tail lights? Forget the tail lights," Julie shouts. "Where's my *trailer*?"

Right or Wrong?

1. Julie likes to go to the beach.
2. She packs her things in the car.
3. She drives up Route 101.
4. She hears a police siren.
5. She pulls over.
6. The officer stays in his car.
7. Julie looks happy.
8. Julie's trailer is missing.

Reading (grammar in context)
Sequencing
True/false statements

9

Study Skills

You're going to practice skimming—reading quickly to find main ideas. Make sure you understand the questions first. Read each article just once, and see how many questions you can answer.

1. How long have people been using wheels?
2. What was the first vehicle with wheels?
3. When were carriages popular?
4. What was the first bicycle made of?
5. Who added foot pedals to the bicycle?
6. How did stagecoaches get their names?
7. What did stagecoaches carry?
8. What was a wagon train?

. . . .

The Wheel Begins to Roll

No one knows for sure who invented the wheel or when. We do know that people used wheels over 5,000 years ago. The first wheels were probably made from logs.

The chariot was the first wheeled vehicle to carry people. It was a two-wheeled cart, open at the back. The ancient Greeks and Romans used chariots in fighting. Chariots were first pulled by donkeys, then by horses.

People Ride Inside

By the 1700s, carriages were popular in Europe and America. They were lightweight and fast, but they weren't very comfortable to ride in. Springs weren't put under the seats until nearly 1800. Roads weren't paved then so it was a very bumpy ride.

Skimming for main ideas
Reading for information
Research

CALLA: Advance organization

routes between cities. The drivers changed horses at certain stops, or "stages" along the way. That's how stagecoaches got their names.

Early Two-wheelers

A Frenchman named Sivrac built a wooden bicycle in 1790. It had no pedals and no handlebars. The rider had to move and steer by putting his feet on the ground and pushing.

A German inventor added handlebars in about 1816. Finally, a Scottish blacksmith named Macmillan added pedals in 1839.

Americans Head West

Coaches were used in Europe for public transportation. When coaches came to America, they carried people, mail, and large packages. The coaches traveled on regular

Pioneers traveled west in covered wagons. Often, everything a family owned was inside, under the high, curved top. Groups of families traveled together in single file. The long line of wagons became known as a wagon train.

CALLA: Advance organization

♪♪ Skimming for main ideas
Reading for information
Research

11

I	me	myself
you	you	yourself
he	him	himself
she	her	herself
it	it	itself
we	us	ourselves
you	you	yourselves
they	them	themselves

1. ★ What's the matter with him?
   ● He hurt himself.

What's the matter with ⎧ her?
⎨ you?
⎩ them?
you two?

2. ★ Please help me.
   ● Oh, you can do it yourself.

Please help ⎧ them.
⎨ us.
⎩ him.

Tom Talker was a know-it-all. He thought a lot of himself. He often said to himself, "Sometimes I'm so smart, I amaze even myself." He also thought he was handsome, and often looked at himself in the mirror.

One day, Tom saw Martha at the store. "Oh, no," Martha thought to herself. Tom walked up to her. "I'm feeling very, very smart today," he said. "Ask me anything."

"Anything?" said Martha. "Hmm. Okay. I'll bet you can't answer my question." "Fine," Tom replied. "And I'll bet you can't answer *my* question."

"What has three legs, flies and talks to itself at night?" asked Martha.

Tom looked puzzled. Finally he said, "I give up. I don't know. What *is* the answer?"

Martha smiled to herself. "I don't know either. But if that's *your* question, I guess I win!"

1. What did Tom often say to himself?
2. What did he often do in front of the mirror?
3. What did Martha say to herself when she saw Tom?
4. What did she do?
5. How did Martha fool Tom?

♪♪ Asking for/giving information (reflexive pronouns)
Reading (grammar in context)
Comprehension/recall questions

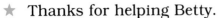

★ Thanks for helping Betty.
● I wasn't helping her.
★ You weren't?
● No, she did it herself.

I thought you were helping Betty, but I was wrong.

Now make conversations with your partner. Be careful!

1.

I thought you were helping Tom, but I was wrong.

2.

I thought you were helping Bill and Ted, but I was wrong.

3.

I thought you were helping Martha, but I was wrong.

4.

I thought you were helping your teacher, but I was wrong.

Practice these conversations with your partner.

1. ★ Can you help me?
   ● Sorry, I can't help you.
     But you can do it yourself.

2. ★ Can you help us?
   ● Sorry, I can't help you.
     But you can do it yourselves.

INTERVIEW

Harry Rowland is the captain of the "Mississippi Queen." Our ESL Reporter is interviewing him.

ESL: Tell us about the "Mississippi Queen," Captain.

R: Well, she's a paddle steamer. She is five decks high. There is a theater and a swimming pool on board.

ESL: How many passengers can the ship take?

R: There are cabins for 400 passengers and a crew of 100.

ESL: And you go up and down the Mississippi?

R: That's right.

ESL: Just how long is the Mississippi?

R: Its 2,348 miles long. It begins in Lake Itasca, Minnesota. It ends in the Gulf of Mexico.

ESL: Is it the longest river in North America?

R: No. The Missouri-Red Rock is longer. It flows into the Mississippi. There are more than 250 other rivers that join the Mississippi. So you could travel tens of thousands of miles and be on rivers the whole time.

ESL: Well, thank you, Captain. This was a very interesting interview.

R: You're welcome.

♫♪

14   Reading/role-playing an interview

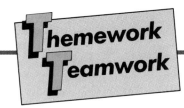

1. Make a map of the United States.
   Draw in the most important rivers.
   Draw in the largest lakes.
   Draw in mountains and deserts.
   Mark with a circle some important cities.

2. Now you have a map, but you have no labels for the map. Instead of writing labels, put numbers next to each thing you have drawn. Then make a number card for each number on your map. Put the number cards in a box. Make a list of the numbers and the names they stand for. Refer to the list when you need to check the right answer.

Play a game with a partner. Exchange maps and number cards. Take turns pulling out number cards. Find the same number on the map and name the place to win a point. Another way you can play is like this:

What number is New York City?

It's number 12.

3. Make a new map of another country or make another map of the United States at home. Play with your family. Keep adding numbers to your first map, and soon you'll be an expert at geography!

Dear Themework,
I now have 78 numbers on my map! I have all the states, but I can't remember all of them yet. My brother is crazy about football. He has all of his favorite teams on his map. My friend Marco has a map of the ports along the Mississippi. Anna has a map of California. She has over 20 cities and towns. She even has highways numbered on her map! We all like adding numbers and playing the game.

Sincerely yours,
Janice Jackson

Read and Do

How to Make a Music Maker

You need: a book, two paper cups, and two rubber bands.

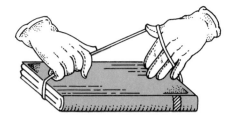 

1. Put a rubber band around a book.

2. Slip a paper cup under the band.

3. Move the cup toward one end. Snap the band. It makes a musical note.

4. Snap the band in another place. Do you get the same sound? Find three different notes by snapping in different places.

5. Slip a bigger or smaller cup under another rubber band.

6. Snap the band. Are the musical notes the same, or different?

7. Get together with friends in a Music Maker band and sing your favorite songs.

Reading and following directions
Music: Listening for pitch changes

The Boy Who Cried Wolf

Once, a shepherd boy was watching his flock of sheep. He got bored, and decided to have some fun.

"Help, help!" he cried. "Wolf! Wolf! The wolves are attacking my sheep."

The people in the village came running to help. The shepherd boy laughed and said, "There are no wolves. I was just fooling." The villagers went back to their work.

But the shepherd boy cried "Wolf! Wolf!" three more times. Three more times, the villagers came running. And three more times the boy laughed. He thought it was a great joke. The villagers did not.

Soon after, some wolves really did come. The shepherd boy cried "Wolf! Wolf!" But the villagers didn't come. The boy ran to the village.

"Help! The wolves are attacking my sheep!" he cried. "You won't fool us again," said the villagers. And so the boy lost all of his sheep.

Liars are not believed, even when they tell the truth.

Listening Comprehension

You are going to listen to some information about gorillas. Listen carefully and complete the sentences below. Write your answers in complete sentences on a separate piece of paper.

1. Gorillas are
   a. a lot like humans.
   b. very different from humans.
   c. just like humans.

2. Gorillas have
   a. the same number of teeth we have.
   b. more teeth than we have.
   c. fewer teeth than we have.

3. Adult males are
   a. shorter than females.
   b. over six feet tall.
   c. under five feet tall.

4. Gorillas live
   a. alone.
   b. in family groups.
   c. in pairs.

5. Gorillas sleep
   a. on the ground.
   b. in trees.
   c. in caves.

6. Gorillas move
   a. every day or two.
   b. every week or two.
   c. every year or two.

Listening for information: factual article
Multiple choice

Reading Comprehension

You are going to read some information about gorillas. Read carefully and answer the questions below. Write your answers in complete sentences on a separate piece of paper.

1. What are four ways gorillas are like humans?
2. What happens to a male gorilla between ten and fourteen years of age?
3. What are the male gorillas called then?
4. What did Koko learn how to do?
5. Why are gorillas in danger?
6. How many gorillas are alive in the jungle today?

Gorillas frown, cry, chuckle, and smile. They even chew their bottom lips when they are nervous. They like to sunbathe with their hands clasped behind their heads.

These unusual animals live about as long as humans do. They live in families, just as humans do. A full-grown male is the head of a family. When a male gorilla is between ten and fourteen years old, the black hair on his back turns gray. These males are then called "silverbacks." The silverbacks decide everything for their families.

Koko is a very famous gorilla. She was raised by humans from the time she was an orphan baby. Scientists taught Koko how to "talk" using sign language. Koko learned over 500 sign language words. She can tell what she wants, how she feels, and even make jokes!

Gorillas are in danger now. They are being hunted and their jungle homes are being cut down. Fewer than 4,000 mountain gorillas are alive in the jungle today. The world of gorillas is getting smaller every year.

Rabbit and Tiger

This is a play. The characters are the Rabbit, the Tiger, and the Farmer. There is also a Storyteller.

(*The storyteller and the characters are on stage.*)

Storyteller: Welcome to our play. Here are the characters.
Rabbit: Hi! I'm the Rabbit.
Tiger: Grr-ah! I'm the Tiger.
Farmer: And I'm the Farmer.

(*The characters leave the stage.*)

Storyteller: The Rabbit and the Tiger are *not* good friends.
Rabbit: (*pops out and laughs*) That's true!
Storyteller: That's because the Tiger is always trying to eat the Rabbit for breakfast, lunch, or dinner.
Tiger: (*pops out and growls*) That's not true!
Storyteller: But the rabbit is always too smart for the Tiger. One day, the Rabbit was sitting by a lake. (*Rabbit enters and sits.*) Soon, a Farmer came by. (*Farmer enters.*)

Literature: play version of Hispanic classic
Shared reading/role-playing
Creative writing

Farmer: Lah, Lah, lah dee dah. Lah, lah. . . Oh, good morning, Rabbit.

Rabbit: Good morning, Farmer. What do you have there?

Farmer: I have some delicious cheese.

Rabbit: And where are you going with that cheese?

Farmer: I'm going to the market in town.

Rabbit: Hmm. Your cheese may spoil before you get there.

Farmer: Do you really think so?

Rabbit: Yes, I do really think so. Let me help you. I'll wrap your cheese in fresh, wet leaves.

Farmer: Well, that's very kind of you. (*The Rabbit leaves the stage and returns with some leaves.*)

Rabbit: Here you are. (*Rabbit gives the leaves to the Farmer.*)

Farmer: And here *you* are. (*The Farmer gives the Rabbit a nice big piece of cheese.*)

Rabbit: Thank you. That's very nice of you.

Farmer: I must go now. Good-bye. (*The Farmer leaves the stage.*)

Rabbit: Good-bye.

Storyteller: The rabbit was enjoying his piece of cheese. . . when the Tiger came by. (*Tiger enters.*)

Tiger: Grr-ah! Now I have you! (*The Rabbit jumps up and pretends to be afraid.*) I'll eat you for lunch!

Rabbit: Well, first have a bite of this delicious cheese.

Tiger: (*Tiger tastes the cheese.*) Mmmmmm-mmm-grr-ah! Where did you get such delicious cheese?

Rabbit: (*pointing off stage*) From the bottom of the lake.

Tiger: (*surprised*) What? Cheese from the bottom of the lake?

Rabbit: Oh, yes. The lake is full of delicious cheese! The best cheese is at the bottom, of course. So I tied two stones to my tail.

Tiger: You tied two stones to your tail?

Rabbit: Yes. And then I jumped in and swam to the bottom.

Tiger: You jumped in and swam to the bottom?

Rabbit: Yes, and I got this delicious cheese.

Tiger: Well, then I will do just the same. (*Tiger exits.*)

Storyteller: As I said, the Rabbit is always too smart for the Tiger. What do you think happens next? (*Pause: Storyteller listens to the audience.*)

Storyteller: Well, this is what happened. The Tiger tied two stones to his tail. He swam to the bottom of the lake. The Rabbit laughed and laughed. As he was laughing, the Farmer came back. (*Farmer enters.*)

Farmer: Rabbit! Rabbit! I saw Tiger heading this way.

Rabbit: I know. No problem.

Farmer: No problem?

Rabbit: Tiger is at the bottom of the lake.

Farmer: At the bottom of the lake? Whatever for?

Rabbit: For a piece of delicious cheese!

Farmer: For a piece of cheese? I don't understand.

Rabbit: Neither does the Tiger. Come on. I'll explain. (*The Farmer and the Rabbit exit.*)

Storyteller: So the Farmer and the Rabbit went off together. They left the poor Tiger at the bottom of the lake. The Tiger nearly drowned, of course. And of course, he didn't find any cheese at the bottom of the lake. Here he comes now.

Tiger: (*sputtering, coughing, and shaking*) Rabbit! Rabbit! Where are you? (*sits and shakes his head*) Grrr-ah! Oh, double Grrr-ah. GRRR-AH! I'll find that Rabbit and have him for dinner if it's the last thing I do! (*curtain*)

2

They're building a
new shopping mall in
Sunnyville. Part of the
mall is finished. The rest
is under construction.

1. Fran Friendly is the architect. She
   drew all the plans. She's talking with
   Rick Moon, the foreman of the
   construction crew.

2. Sara Spark is the master electrician.
   She's installing a big neon sign.

3. Dan Rogers is the master plumber.
   He's putting in pipes.

Social studies: community life
Asking for/giving information
Identifying/describing

4. Blanca Velez is the master bricklayer. She's building a brick wall around the fountain.

5. Clint Westwood is the master carpenter. He's working on the roof.

6. June Moon is the master painter. She's painting the inside of the mall.

Social studies: community life
Asking for/giving information
Identifying/describing

25

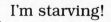

DATA BANK

Yogurt
Strawberry, chocolate,
vanilla, peach, pineapple

Fresh Juice
carrot, orange,
grapefruit, apple

Snacks/Sandwiches
egg salad, cheese, peanut
butter, hot dog, hamburger

Food
Role-playing fixed and free dialogues
Creating new dialogues from cues

Say the right thing!

Are you hungry?
I'm starving.

Me too.
Yes, I'm famished.

How about a snack?
Let's have lunch.

Okay.
Sounds good.

What do you want to eat?
What do you want to drink?

I'll have a glass of juice.
I want an egg salad sandwich.

I hate eggs. I'll have a hot dog.
Apple or orange juice?

Apple.
Okay, let's order.

Now make conversations with your partner. Begin with these situations.

1. You say that you're hungry.
   Your friend says she's starving.
   You order a hot dog and a lemonade.
   She orders a cheese sandwich and milk.
   You decide to get take-out.
   You lend your friend a dollar.

2. The waitress asks what you want.
   You want a frozen yogurt.
   She asks what flavor.
   You choose chocolate.
   The yogurt is 80 cents.
   You give the waitress a dollar.

Role-playing fixed dialogues
Understanding sequence in conversations
Creating new dialogues from cues

27

Pair Practice 1

fast	faster	fastest	big	bigger	biggest
slow	slower	slowest	hot	hotter	hottest
old	older	oldest	sad	sadder	saddest

happy	happier	happiest	exciting	more exciting	most exciting
funny	funnier	funniest	boring	more boring	most boring
silly	sillier	silliest	delicious	more delicious	most delicious

good	better	best
bad	worse	worst

Practice conversations like these with your partner.

1. ★ Is your bike fast?
   ● Yes, it is.
   ★ Is it faster than my bike?
   ● Yes! It's the fastest bike in the world!

2. ★ Is your brother silly?
   ● Yes, he is.
   ★ Is he sillier than my brother?
   ● Yes. He's the silliest brother in the world!

3. ★ Is your book exciting?
   ● Yes, it is.
   ★ Is it more exciting than my book?
   ● Yes! It's the most exciting book in the world!

Asking for/giving information (comparatives/superlatives)
Role-playing fixed and free dialogues
Spelling regular word endings

Jerry was on vacation. He felt very happy. He rented the smallest, cheapest car he could find. He started driving on the highway, but he didn't like it. "This is the straightest most boring road in the world," he thought to himself.

So he drove off the highway. He found a narrow, curving road. "This is better," he thought. He drove through pretty villages. "These are the prettiest villages in the world," he thought. He stopped and talked to friendly people. "These are the friendliest people in the world," he thought. The road became narrower and slower. Jerry felt happier and happier.

Suddenly a huge truck came around a curve. The driver leaned out of the window and shouted, "PIG!" Jerry couldn't have been more surprised. "That's the unfriendliest person in the world," he thought. "And PIG to you," he shouted back. He drove around the curve. He slammed on his brakes. In the middle of the road was the biggest pig in the world!

1. What kind of car did Jerry rent?
2. Why didn't he like the highway?
3. What kind of road did he find?
4. How did he feel?
5. What did he think about the villages?
6. What did he think about the people?
7. What did he think about the driver?
8. What was in the middle of the road?

Study Skills

Read the true/false statements. Skim the articles to decide which statements are true and which are false. Answer what you know after only one quick reading. Then scan the articles—read for details—to finish deciding which statements are true or false.

1. Bell invented the telephone in 1886.
2. There are more than 400 million telephones in the United States.
3. Edison invented the phonograph.
4. The Wright Brothers' first flight took place in 1903.
5. Their plane was called "Flyer 1."
6. The pilot sat in the middle.
7. The longest flight was 12 seconds.
8. Charles Darrow was unemployed in 1930.
9. Darrow invented a new board game.
10. Darrow bought a huge factory.

Inventions and Inventors

What would our lives be like without people who invent—create—totally new things? Did you know that the wheel is an essential part of clocks, trains, bikes, washing machines—even the telephone?

Hello?

Alexander Graham Bell invented the telephone in 1876. He was trying to invent a hearing aid for deaf people.

Today, there are more than 400 million telephones in the world! The average American makes about 1,000 calls a year.

Lights in the Dark

Thomas Alva Edison is probably the best-known inventor. He invented the first light bulb in 1879. He also invented the phonograph

Reading for information
Research
True/false statements

CALLA: Selective attention
Transfer
Inferencing

and an early motion picture machine. Edison and his helpers invented over 1,000 useful things.

The First Flight

Orville and Wilbur Wright invented the first successful airplane.

Orville took their plane, named "Flyer 1," up in the air in 1903. It flew for 12 seconds. Orville had to lie down to fly the plane. He balanced it by moving his hips.

Wilbur took the plane up on the fourth flight of the day. It stayed in the air for 59 seconds. But a gust of wind knocked it over and wrecked it after landing.

It was the last flight of "Flyer 1." But the two brothers had opened the door to a whole new age.

Gamesmanship

In 1930, there was a terrible period in the United States called the Great Depression. Millions of people were unemployed, homeless, and hungry.

Charles Darrow was an out-of-work engineer. One night, he got an idea for a game based on buying and selling things. He played with his neighbors, and improved the rules and the spaces on the board.

Darrow began to manufacture the game himself. He made his basement into the first factory to produce "Monopoly." "Monopoly" is one of the most popular board games of all time. Darrow became a millionaire many times over.

CALLA: Selective attention
    Transfer
    Inferencing

hear	hears	heard		take	takes	took
see	sees	saw		come	comes	came
run	runs	ran		tell	tells	told
drive	drives	drove		stand	stands	stood
say	says	said		bring	brings	brought

It was a quiet day. Suddenly a police officer heard a scream. She ran around the corner. She couldn't believe her eyes. There was a man with a huge lion on a leash. "Hey, you!" she said. "You can't walk around the streets with a lion. Take it to the zoo!"

"Okay, officer. I just wanted to show Baby the town." The man opened the door of his car and the lion jumped in. The officer stood and stared as the man drove off in the direction of the zoo.

The next day, the police officer saw the same man and the same lion again. "Hey you!" she said. "Come over here! And bring that lion with you!" The man brought the lion over to the officer.

"What's the problem, officer?" "Problem? I told you yesterday to take that lion to the zoo!"

"Oh, I did, officer. I took Baby to the zoo. He enjoyed it very much. But today, I'm taking him to the movies!"

Understanding irregular verbs
Reading (grammar in context)

*Take turns with your partner. Read the sentences aloud
and choose the right form of the verb.*

1. ★ Do you think she is nice?
   ● Yes, I (think, thinks) she is
     very nice.

2. ★ What kind of car do they
     drive?
   ● They (drive, drives) a van.

3. ★ What does he take to school?
   ● He (takes, take) the bus.

4. ★ Where does she run?
   ● She (run, runs) in the park.

5. We (bring, brings) our lunch to
   school.

6. He (says, say) hello.

7. They (stands, stand) in line.

8. I (hear, hears) the bell.

9. (Do, does) you like milk?

10. (Don't, doesn't) he eat meat?

11. (Do, does) she feel happy?

12. I (don't, doesn't) drive a car.

13. We (don't, doesn't) like eggs.

14. They (do, does) like eggs.

INTERVIEW

Barbara Brown works at one of the biggest museums in the country. She's an expert on dinosaurs. Our ESL Reporter is interviewing her.

ESL: What sort of animals were dinosaurs?

B: They were reptiles. They were the same family as turtles, snakes, lizards, and crocodiles.

ESL: Were they all the same?

B: No, there were many kinds of dinosaurs. Some were meat-eaters. Some were plant-eaters. Some walked on two legs; some walked on four legs.

ESL: And they were all huge, weren't they?

B: Actually, no. Some of the first dinosaurs were no bigger than a lizard.

ESL: The iguana lizard looks like a small dinosaur.

B: That's right. It does.

ESL: How big were the meat-eating dinosaurs?

B: The biggest were about 90 feet long from head to tail. They had front legs that were just like short, weak arms.

ESL: Tell us something about the plant-eaters.

B: Some of them lived in swamps. They had long necks, but their heads were very small. Some were huge, weighing over 50 tons. That is 17 times more than a full-grown elephant weighs.

ESL: Wow!

  Reading/role-playing an interview

1. Find out the names of five different dinosaurs.
   Did they walk or swim?
   What did they eat?
   Where did they live?
   How long ago did they live?
   How big were they?
   How long ago did they disappear?

2. Work with a partner. Make a mural or a table-top display of dinosaurs. Cut out pictures, draw, or make clay models of your favorites. Write down the information you found. Were other animals alive at the same time? If so, add them to your project. Were people alive then? If so, tell how they lived.

3. Organize your information for an oral report. Try to answer *Who, What, Where, When, How* and *How long* questions when you present your report.

Dear Themework,

My sister and I are in the same class. We made a huge mural. It stretched all the way around the classroom. Two friends of mine helped us too. The librarian helped us find some interesting books on flying dinosaurs. I copied out the facts and made labels for the mural. It looked really neat. We had fun making it, and we also got a good grade!

Yours truly,
Li Ann Chang

Problem Solving

Mrs. Comb   Miss Bunn   Mr. Pill   Mr. Apple   Miss Rose

There are five small businesses on Main Street. The business owners are: Mrs. Comb, who is not the hairdresser, Miss Bunn, who is not the baker, Mr. Pill, who is not the pharmacist, Mr. Apple who is not the grocer, and Miss Rose, who is not the florist.

Miss Rose owns a business on the end. Mr. Pill's business is the next to the grocer's. He's very friendly with the baker. He hopes she will sell him her business one day.

Who owns each business?

Miss Rose is not the florist, but her business is on one end. So she must be the hairdresser. Mr. Pill is not the pharmacist, but his business is next to the grocer's. So he must be the florist. The baker is a woman, but it isn't Miss Bunn. So it must be Mrs. Comb. Mr. Apple is not the grocer, so he must be the pharmacist. That leaves Miss Bunn, who must be the grocer.

The Meal

Timothy Tompkins had turnips and tea.
The turnips were tiny.
He ate at least three.
And then, for dessert,
He had onions and ice.
He liked that so much
That he ordered it twice.
He had two cups of ketchup,
A prune, and a pickle.
"Delicious," said Timothy.
"Well worth a nickel."
He folded his napkin
And hastened to add,
"It's one of the loveliest breakfasts I've had."

Karla Kuskin

Listening Comprehension

You are going to listen to the first part of a famous story. Listen carefully and complete the sentences below. Write your answers on a separate piece of paper.

1. Once there was a town called
   a. Europe.
   b. Hamelin.
   c. Hotdog.

2. The only thing wrong was
   a. it was full of cats.
   b. it was full of children.
   c. it was full of rats.

3. The people went to the
   a. mayor.
   b. council.
   c. police.

4. One day,
   a. a strange man came to town.
   b. a strange woman came to town.
      a strange animal came to town.

5. The stranger offered
   a. to run for mayor.
   b. to kill the rats.
   c. to get rid of the rats.

6. In return, the mayor would
   a. give him a medal.
   b. give him money.
   c. give him a house.

Listening for information
Literature: The Pied Piper of Hamelin
Multiple choice

Reading Comprehension

You are going to read the next part of the story of "The Pied Piper of Hamelin." Read carefully and answer the questions below. Write your answers in full sentences on a separate piece of paper.

1. What did the Piper wear?
2. What did the Piper play?
3. Where did he begin to play?
4. What did the rats do?
5. Where did the Piper lead the rats?
6. What happened to the rats?
7. What did the people do?
8. What did the mayor do?
9. What did the Piper warn the mayor?
10. What did the Piper do then?

The Pied Piper was a strange-looking man. He wore a tall, pointed hat, and a long, flowing cape. He played a long, shiny flute. The Piper began to play in the town square.

Rats came running from everywhere. They came out of the houses and the shops. The Pied Piper played up and down the streets. Everywhere he went, the rats followed him. The Pied Piper led the rats to the river. The rats all jumped into the river and drowned.

The people cheered. They were happy to be rid of the rats. But the mayor changed his mind about the money. He refused to give any money at all to the Pied Piper. "Give me the money you promised," he said. "If you don't, I'll play a different tune you will *not* like," he warned. But the mayor still refused. The Pied Piper picked up his flute and began to play a new tune.

What do you think happened next? Make up your own ending.

Reading for information/predicting/creative writing
Literature: The Pied Piper of Hamelin
Answering information questions

39

Through the Looking Glass

Excerpted from the book by Lewis Carroll

Humpty Dumpty was sitting on the top of a high wall. Alice wondered how he could keep his balance.

"How exactly like an egg he is," Alice said aloud.

"It's very *provoking*," Humpty Dumpty said after a long silence, "to be called an egg."

"I said you *looked* like an egg, Sir. Some eggs are very pretty, you know. And what a beautiful belt you've got on! At least, a beautiful tie, I should have said—no, a belt, I mean . . ."

She stopped. Humpty Dumpty looked very angry. He said nothing for a minute or two.

"It is a—*most—provoking—thing*," he said at last, "when a person doesn't know a necktie from a belt!"

"I know it's very ignorant of me," Alice said. (If only I knew, she thought, which is his neck and which is his waist!)

"It's a tie, child, and a beautiful one as you say. It's a present from the White King and Queen. They gave it to me," he continued, "for an un-birthday present."

"What *is* an un-birthday present?"

"A present given when it isn't your birthday, of course."

Alice thought a little. "I like birthday presents best," she said at last.

"You don't know what you're talking about! How many days are there in a year?"

Literature: classic story

"Three hundred and sixty-five."

"And how many birthdays do you have?"

"One."

"And so, there are three hundred and sixty-four days a year when you might get un-birthday presents. And only *one* for birthday presents!"

Humpty Dumpty recited a poem for Alice. Then she felt she should be going.

"Good-bye, till we meet again!" she said.

"I wouldn't know you again if we *did* meet. You're exactly like other people."

"Your face is the same as everybody's—two eyes, nose in the middle, mouth under. Now, if you had the two eyes on the same side of the nose . . . or the mouth at the top—that would be *some* help."

"It wouldn't look very nice," Alice objected. But Humpty Dumpty only shut his eyes and said, "Wait till you've tried."

Alice walked quietly away. She couldn't help saying to herself, "Of all the unsatisfactory—(She repeated this. It was a great feeling to have such a long word to say.) "Of all the *unsatisfactory* people I *ever* met—" She never finished the sentence. Suddenly a heavy crash shook the forest from end to end.

There are twenty men and women on the Sunnyville Police Force. The Police Force keeps law and order in Sunnyville.

1. Betty Blue is the Chief of Police. Bart Star is the Deputy Chief.

2. Some police officers ride in squad cars. They patrol the neighborhoods.

3. Some officers ride on motorcycles. They patrol the highways.

4. Some officers ride on horses. They patrol the parks and beaches.

5. Some officers direct traffic.

6. Maxine Ring is the radio dispatcher. If there is an emergency, people dial 911 and Maxine answers right away. She sends officers to help.

♪♪ Social studies: community life
Asking for/giving information
Role-playing   45

Life Skills

Asking for/giving directions
Role-playing fixed dialogues

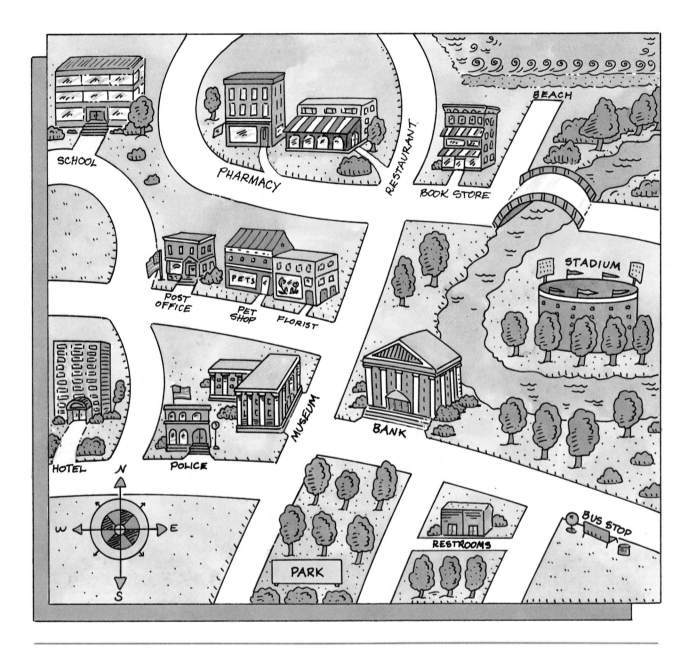

Work with your partner. Take turns asking for directions and giving directions "to" and "from."

1. From the hotel to the bookstore.
2. From the Post Office to the bus stop.
3. From the pharmacy to the bank.
4. From the bus stop to the Police Station.
5. From the school to the museum.
6. From the bridge to the restrooms.
7. From the florist to the park.
8. From the beach to the hotel.

	have to work now.	We	have to work now.
I	had to work yesterday.	You	had to work yesterday.
	will have to work tomorrow.	They	will have to work tomorrow.

He	has to work now.
She	had to work yesterday.
It	will have to work tomorrow.

A new boss came to Ace Mattress Factory. She was very strict. She said to the secretary, "You have to keep a record of what happens every day. You have to write down everything."

The next day, the boss found a worker sleeping on a mattress. She took the worker to her office. "Write this down," she said to the secretary. "Worker was sleeping on a mattress."

"Do I have to write that?" the secretary asked.

"Yes," replied the boss, "You have to."

"But I'm a mattress tester." said the worker. "I have to rest when I test. Does he really have to write that down?"

"He has to," said the boss.

"Don't worry," said the secretary. "I just got an idea."

The next day, the boss looked at the secretary's record book. She was very angry. "What's the meaning of this?"

The secretary read from the record book: "The boss was not asleep on a mattress today." He smiled at the boss. "Well, it was true, wasn't it? So I had to write it down."

Understanding/expressing obligation
Reading (grammar in context)

1. ★ I'm sorry, I can't play now.
   ● Why not?
   ★ I have to go to the dentist.

2. ★ Jack can't play today.
   ● Why not?
   ★ He has to go to the florist.

3. ★ I couldn't play yesterday.
   ● Why not?
   ★ I had to go to the library.

4. ★ Jack couldn't play yesterday.
   ● Why not?
   ★ He had to go to the store.

*Work with your partner. Make conversations from the
information below.*

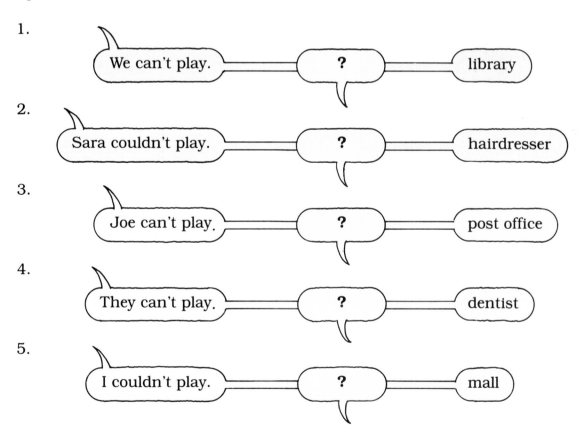

1. We can't play. — ? — library

2. Sara couldn't play. — ? — hairdresser

3. Joe can't play. — ? — post office

4. They can't play. — ? — dentist

5. I couldn't play. — ? — mall

Study Skills

Read the true/false sentences. Then skim the articles. How many sentences can you correctly identify as true or false after just one reading?

1. Susan B. Anthony was an American.
2. She fought for women's rights.
3. All woman could vote when Susan B. Anthony died.
4. Lindbergh was the first man to fly.
5. He flew across the Atlantic in 1927.
6. Lindbergh had good weather.
7. Amelia Earhart flew the same route as Lindbergh.
8. Earhart died somewhere in the Pacific.

. . . .

Famous Firsts

Maybe you have heard about some of these people and places. Each person did something important—something heroic first.

Men only

Susan B. Anthony was born in the U.S. in the 1800s. At that time, only men could vote in elections. Susan B. Anthony thought women should be able to vote, too. She spent her life fighting to get women the right to vote. She voted in 1872, but her vote wasn't counted. Moreover, she was arrested. When she died in 1906, only four states had given women the right to vote. Today, every woman in every state has that right.

BRADY, PHOTO., NEW YORK.

Reading for information
Research
True/false statements

CALLA: Transfer
Self-evaluation

One Way to Paris

Charles Lindbergh was the first person to fly alone across the Atlantic Ocean. A New York City hotel owner had offered a $25,000 prize to the first person who could fly non-stop from New York to Paris. Lindbergh took off early in the morning of May 20, 1927. He flew his plane, "The Spirit of St. Louis," through rain, fog, and sleet. He landed in Paris 33 hours and 30 minutes later. He had flown 3,600 miles alone across the Atlantic.

Female Flyer Makes News

Amelia Earhart was the first woman—and the second pilot—to fly across the Atlantic alone. To prepare for the long flight, she went without food or sleep for many days at a time. Her flight from Newfoundland to Ireland took 14 hours.

In 1937, she and Fred Noonan were trying to fly a two-engine plane around the world. Over the Pacific, they ran short of fuel. Ships and planes searched for the couple, but no trace of them or their plane was ever found.

I have changed. But I have always had brown hair.

You have changed. But you have always had blue eyes.

He has changed. But he has always had big feet.

She has changed. But she has always had pretty hair.

We have changed. But we have always had big ears.

You two have changed. But you have always had black hair.

They have changed. But they have always had good teeth.

Mario was at a party. He saw a girl across the room. He was sure she was an old friend. He walked over to her.

"Hello! It's good to see you again."

"But I . . ."

"You have changed the color of your hair. You had black hair when I last saw you."

"No, I have always had brown hair."

"Really? And you have started wearing glasses."

"But I have always had glasses."

"And you have changed your teeth."

"No, don't be ridiculous. I have always had these teeth."

"It's good to see you, Eleanor."

"Eleanor? But my name is Jean."

"Oh, I see. You have changed your name, too!"

Describing physical characteristics
Reading (grammar in context)

1. ★ Tom has changed, hasn't he?
   ● What do you mean?
   ★ Well, he is tall now.
   ● But Tom has always been tall.

2. ★ Frank and Jane have changed, haven't they?
   ● What do you mean?
   ★ Well, they wear glasses now
   ● But they have always worn glasses.

Work with your partner. Make conversations from the information below.

1. Sara is thin now.

2. Fred is handsome now.

3. Betty and Bart are strong now.

4. We are happy now.

5. Max is funny now.

6. You wear glasses now.

7. I wear jeans now.

8. You wear hats now.

INTERVIEW

D avid Dunn works for the United Nations. He's an expert on agriculture. Our ESL Reporter is interviewing him.

ESL: What sort of farming do you specialize in?

D: Well, mainly groundnuts.

ESL: Groundnuts?

D: Oh, you probably call them peanuts.

ESL: Oh, I love peanuts! But aren't they from North America?

D: Some, yes. But peanuts grow all over the world these days. Originally, Spanish explorers discovered peanuts when they were looking for gold in South America. They weren't very impressed by the nuts, but they took them back to Europe anyhow.

ESL: So peanuts come from South America?

D: Yes. And from Europe, the nut went to Africa, China, and India. Later, slaves from Africa took the nuts with them to North America.

ESL: Are peanuts an important cash crop?

D: Yes. In the United States, peanuts are grown on large plantations. In 1987, over 44 million pounds of peanuts were grown!

ESL: Do they grow easily?

D: Fairly easily. They need a good climate with moderate rainfall, much sunshine, and warm temperatures.

ESL: How long does it take them to grow?

D: Between 130 and 150 days. First, small yellow flowers appear after a month. Then come the seed pods. The pods bury themselves in the ground. The nuts themselves grow under the ground.

ESL: So that's why you call them groundnuts!

D: Right!

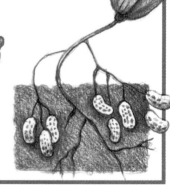

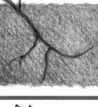

1. What do you know about the United Nations? When did the organization start? How many nations were there at first? How many nations are there now? What is the General Assembly? What is the Security Council? What do you think the United Nations should do for the future?

2. Work with four friends to form a small "United Nations." Choose five countries as members. Choose one project that your countries will support. Tell how you will make the world a better place.

3. Research the country you represent in your "United Nations." Where is it? How big is it? How many people live there? What food is grown there? What kind of government does it have? Organize your information for an oral report.

4. What do you know about the slave trade? Who took slaves? Where did they take the slaves from? Where were the slaves sent? Why? When did slave trading stop? Did it stop at the same time all over the world? Are there slaves today?

Dear Themework,

My friends and I formed a United Nations. At first, it was hard choosing just five countries. But finally, we chose the United States, Canada, Mexico, Vietnam, and China. Our project was world hunger. We found out a lot more about peanuts and things made from peanuts. All our food packages have peanuts, wheat, milk, and rice. Next week I'm going to give an oral report on Vietnam.

Yours,
Larry Smith

Read and Do

How to Make a Piggy Bank

You need: four pages of newspaper, paste, glue, an orange,
four toothpaste tube tops, a cork, and some paint.

1. Tear the newspaper into small pieces. Put the pieces in a bowl of water and let them soak.

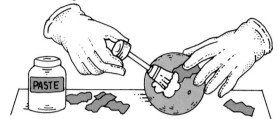

2. Press a piece of paper on the orange. Put paste all over it. Cover the orange with at least six layers of paper.

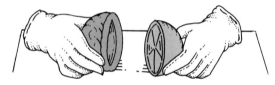

3. Put the orange someplace warm to dry. Then cut the orange in half, and take out the inside.

4. Cut a slot in one half, and then glue the two halves back together.

5. Cover the ball with two more layers of paper and paste. Let the ball dry again.

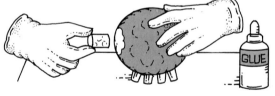

6. Glue the four toothpaste tops to the ball for legs. Glue the cork on as a nose.

7. Paint your piggy bank any way you like. And save your money!

The Lion and The Mouse

One day, the Lion was sleeping. The Mouse ran across the Lion's paws. The Lion woke up, and was angry. He grabbed the Mouse and opened his huge jaws.

"Don't eat me!" the Mouse begged. "Please! I'm sorry. Let me go, and maybe someday, I can help you in some way." The Lion laughed. "How could you help *me*?" But he let the Mouse go.

Some time later, the Mouse heard the Lion roaring angrily. The Mouse ran to see what was wrong. The Lion was caught in a hunter's net.

The Mouse said, "Don't worry. I'll get you out of there." He began to nibble on the net. He nibbled and nibbled, and finally, there was a hole in the net. The Lion squeezed through the hole. He was free again. "Thank you, Mouse." "You're welcome, Lion. And let this be a lesson to you."

Little friends can be big friends.

Listening Comprehension

You are going to listen to some information about lions. Listen carefully, and take notes. Then answer the questions below. Write your answers in complete sentences on a separate piece of paper.

1. What is a family group of lions called?
2. How many lions can be in a group?
3. Who does most of the hunting?
4. What is the top speed of a lion?
5. How far can a grown lion leap?

Listening for information: factual article
Information questions

You are going to read some information about lions. Read carefully and decide whether the sentences below are true or false. Rewrite the false sentences to make them true. Write your answers on a separate piece of paper.

1. Lions are found in Africa and China.
2. Lions live longer in the wild than they do in captivity.
3. Male lions are the head of prides.
4. Male lions protect the pride while the females hunt.
5. Male lions are about eight feet long.
6. Female lions are a little shorter than male lions.
7. Baby lions are called cubs.

    The lion is known as "The King of the Beasts." Lions are found in wildlife reserves in Africa. They also live in one part of India. Like humans, lions live in families. In the wild, lions live about eleven years. They live twice as long in captivity, however.

    A family group, called a *pride*, is headed by a male lion. Other grown males may be in a pride, but only one lion is "the boss." The females do almost all the hunting. "The boss" guards the rest of the pride and babysits the young lions.

    Lions are big and strong. Male lions average over nine feet in length and weigh about 400 pounds. Female lions average eight feet and 300 pounds. Females have two to four babies at a time. These cubs like to wrestle and run. This strengthens them for hunting when they grow up. A lion that can't hunt will starve. A favorite meal of the lion is the wildebeest. Wildebeests are very fast, and often outrun the lions. But in the end, the lions catch and kill them. That's the law of nature.

George Washington Carver

George Washington Carver was born in Missouri at the
beginning of the Civil War. His mother was a slave, so George
was a slave, too. Slavery is against the law in the United
States today. But it wasn't against the law when George was
born. George was owned by a white man, a farmer named
Moses Carver. He was called "Carver's George."

After the Civil War, slaves became free. George could have
left the Carver farm. But he didn't. He wanted to stay. Moses
Carver's wife taught him to read and write.

♪♪ Literature: historical biography
Shared reading
Creative writing

When George was fourteen years old, he went to school for the first time. He took the name George Carver. He already knew how to do many things. He knew how to make shoes, candles, quilts, and clothes. He knew how to knit and crochet. He knew how to plant and raise vegetables and flowers. But he wanted to learn more.

School was not free. George worked hard to earn the money to pay for his education. He worked as a cook. He washed and ironed clothes. He took care of people's houses and gardens. And he studied hard. He went to college and studied agriculture. He graduated from college in Iowa in 1894. After graduation, he worked for the college. He was in charge of the greenhouse. Scientists were trying to grow stronger, healthier plants. George concentrated on the peanut.

Two years later, a famous black educator named Booker T. Washington offered George a job. The job was at a new college for black students in Tuskeegee, Alabama. The job was teaching agriculture.

Almost all the students were sons and daughters of poor farmers. The farmers were still growing cotton. Cotton was the crop they had always grown—since the time they were slaves. George tried to teach the children of these farmers how to grow peanuts. Cotton robbed the soil of food. Peanuts didn't. Peanuts put food back into the soil. Little by little, farmers began to grow peanuts.

Literature: historical biography

George Washington Carver continued to study and research uses of the peanut. He spent the rest of his life at Tuskeegee Institute. He helped poor farmers improve their land. He helped them to change from growing only cotton. He never became rich; he never became really famous. But he helped change a whole way of life in the American south. George Washington Carver died in 1943.

The work of George Washington Carver lives on. Today, peanuts and by-products of peanuts are used to make many, many things.

food for people

soaps and shaving creams

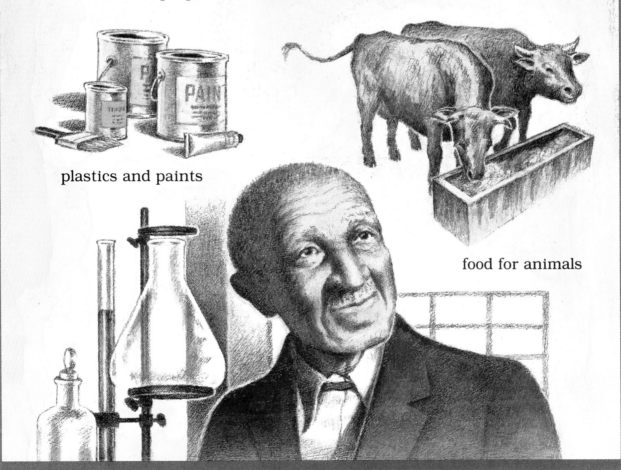

plastics and paints

food for animals

Sunnyville has one hospital. There are also two clinics in Sunnyville, and there is one veterinarian. The Emergency Room of the hospital is open twenty-four hours a day.

1. Last week, there was an accident at the construction site. June Moon fell off a ladder. The foreman called 911 and an ambulance came right away. The ambulance crew took June to the Emergency Room.

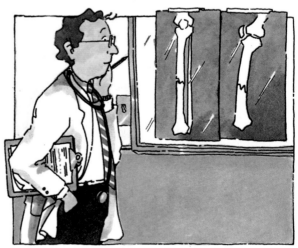

2. A doctor examined June. He decided to take x-rays of her leg.

3. He studied the x-rays. June's leg was broken.

Social studies: community life
Describing health/actions/scenes
Asking for/giving information

4. They took June to the operating room. They set her leg in a cast.

5. June rested in the hospital for a few days.

She learned how to walk with crutches.

Her friends came to visit her. They all signed her cast.

June's cast has to be on for about six weeks. Then the doctor will examine her leg again.

Social studies: community life
Describing health/actions/scenes
Asking for/giving information

65

Hello?

I'm sorry, Rosa. He's not at home.

Certainly. What's your number?

944-3700. I'll give him the message.

Hello, is Andy there? This is Rosa.

Will you ask him to call me?

It's 944-3700.

Thanks. Bye.

Good morning. State Bank. Can I help you?

That line is busy. Will you hold?

Mr. Rogers, please.

No, I'll call back later.

DATA BANK

Operator.
Can I help you?
That line is busy.
Will you hold?
area code
information
Dial. . .

Is Pam there?
Can I speak to Pam?
Is Pam home?

Mr. Rogers, please.

Can I leave a message?
I'll call back later.
Please have him call me.

Talking on the telephone
Role-playing fixed and free dialogues
Creating new dialogues from cues

Say the right thing!

Information. What city please?
Operator. Can I help you? ········· Riverside, California?
The number for Max Shorter, please?

Sorry. That's out of my area.
Max Carter? ········· No, Shorter. S-h-o-r-t-e-r.
How do I get a number in Riverside?

Dial 1, the area code, and 555-1212.
The number is 388-0191. ········· But I don't know the area code.
Do I have to dial 1 first?

Yes, you do.
It's 203. ········· Thanks.
Thank you.

Now make conversations with your partner.
Begin with these situations.

1. You call a friend. Her brother says she isn't at home. You say who you are and leave your number. The brother repeats your number. You thank him and say good-bye.

2. You call your mother at work. The operator says her line is busy. You say you'll hold. The operator says the line is still busy. You leave a message.

Role-playing fixed dialogues
Understanding sequence in conversations
Creating new dialogues from cues

67

Pair Practice 1

Vowel plus y = ys		Consonant plus y = ies		f or fe = ves	
day	days	baby	babies	calf	calves
key	keys	story	stories	half	halves
boy	boys	library	libraries	knife	knives
monkey	monkeys	candy	candies	wife	wives

o = os or oes		words that don't follow the rules			
tomato	tomatoes	child	children	man	men
potato	potatoes	foot	feet	woman	women
piano	pianos	tooth	teeth	mouse	mice
radio	radios	goose	geese	fish	fish

Work with your partner. Take turns asking and answering the questions. Begin your answers with There was *or* There were.

1. How many monkeys were in the zoo?
2. How many lions were there?
3. How many geese were there?
4. How many boys were there?
5. How many women were there?
6. How many children were there?

68   Understanding plural nouns
Asking for/giving information
Spelling regular noun plurals

Ali Baba and the Forty Thieves

Ali Baba was such a poor man that he had only one shoe for his two feet. Even the mice in his house were hungry.

One day, his wife said, "We have no food in the house. No rice. No potatoes. Go and collect leaves in the forest so that I can make a soup."

Ali was a lazy man. He looked for leaves for about ten minutes and then he climbed a tree to sleep. He was afraid of wolves. When he woke up he was surprised to see forty thieves on forty horses. They stopped in front of a big rock.

"Open Sesame!" shouted the leader. A door in the rock opened. The thieves carried sacks full of gold into the cave. When they had finished, the leader shouted,

"Close Sesame!" and the door closed. As soon as the thieves had disappeared, Ali Baba jumped down from the tree, said, "Open Sesame" and went into the cave.

There were shelves all around the walls. The shelves were full of sacks. The sacks were full of gold. Ali took a sack home with him.

Unfortunately, one of the thieves saw Ali's footprints in the sand. He followed them to Ali's home. He took out his knife and made a cross on the door.

"Now I shall know which house it is," he said.

He rode off to get the other thieves. But Ali had seen the thief.

He and his wife took brooms and swept away the footprints. Then he made crosses on every door in the street. When the forty thieves arrived they had their knives between their teeth. But they never found Ali—or the gold. And Ali and his wife lived happily ever after.

Study Skills

Read the true/false statements. Then skim the articles just once. How many answers are you sure of after just one reading?

1. The Chinese sent up the first rockets.
2. The Russians were first in outer space.
3. Goddard's rocket went up in 1957.
4. The British settled New York first.
5. The Dutch bought New Amsterdam from the British.
6. Seward was Czar of Russia.
7. Most people thought Alaska was valuable.
8. Bees sting when they are hungry.
9. Piranhas are more dangerous than sharks.
10. There is no such thing as a vampire bat.

Rockets and Space

Was the United States the first country to send a rocket into space? No. Robert Goddard, an American scientist, sent up a rocket in 1926. It traveled as high as a 20-story building, but it didn't reach outer space. Outer space begins about 100 miles above the earth. The first rocket to reach outer space was launched by the Soviet Union in 1957.

But the very first rockets were launched in the year 1200 or so. Where? In China. The rockets were like the rockets we use for fireworks.

Reading for information
Research
True/false statements

Great Land Deals

The first settlers in what is now New York City were from Holland. They bought the land from the Manhattan Indians for goods worth less than $100! They named their settlement New Amsterdam.

The British didn't pay anything in terms of money for the land. They took over the colony in 1664 and renamed it New York.

Perhaps the very best land deal was made by William Seward. Seward was the American Secretary of State. In 1867, he bought all of Alaska from Czar Nicholas the Second of Russia. He paid only two cents an acre. Nicholas thought the land was worthless. The Russians had already explored the land and killed most of the animals for their fur. Most Americans thought Alaska was useless wilderness, too. They didn't think Seward had made a bargain at all. They called his great land deal "Seward's Folly." Later, huge deposits of oil and minerals were found in Alaska.

Animal Facts

Do you think that bees are mean and sting you on purpose? They don't. Bees sting only when they are threatened. So don't bother a bee, and it won't bother you!

Is the shark the most dangerous fish? No, piranhas are. These small fish have very sharp teeth. They travel in schools of thousands and attack all at once. Piranhas can eat a large fish or animal—even a human—in just minutes. So don't go swimming in the Amazon.

You cannot get warts from a toad. Snakes are not slimy; their skins are dry. Bats are not blind. Vampire bats live in Central and South America. They rarely attack humans; they prefer cattle and birds.

Pair Practice 2

keep	keeps	kept	leave	leaves	left
say	says	said	think	thinks	thought
build	builds	built	feel	feels	felt
send	sends	sent	sink	sinks	sank

Take turns with your partner. Read the sentences aloud and choose the right form of the verb.

1. My father (feel, feels) great today.
2. I (leaves, leave) for school at 8.
3. "Hey!" the officer (say, said).
4. Does the farmer (keep, keeps) pigs?
5. I (feels, feel) just so so today.
6. My mom (sleep, sleeps) late on Sunday.
7. Yesterday he (feels, felt) sick.
8. Did you (build, built) that house?
9. When did he (find, found) the money?
10. Did you (thought, think) about me?
11. Did they (left, leave) late?
12. What did you (thought, think) about it?

Understanding irregular verbs
Choosing correct verb forms in context

Don, Wayne, and Warren were shipwrecked. Their ship sank in the Pacific Ocean. They found themselves on a desert island. They built a small hut and slept inside. They found food and water. They thought, "We'll be rescued soon."

But they weren't rescued. They left messages in the sand. They sent messages in bottles. Still, they weren't rescued. "Don't worry," Don said to his friends. But they felt worse and worse. They all thought about going home.

One day, Wayne found another bottle on the beach. He rubbed the sand off of it—and a genie jumped out! "Oh, what a relief!" the genie said. "I have been captive in that bottle for 10,000 years. Now that I'm free, I will give you three wishes."

"That means we can have one wish each," Warren said. "Well, I wish to be sent home immediately."

"Your wish is my command," said the genie. He waved his hand, and Warren disappeared.

"Wow! I want the same wish," said Wayne. "Your wish is my command," said the genie. And Wayne disappeared.

"Your turn," the genie said to Don.

"Gee, I'm not sure," Don answered. "Suddenly I felt so lonely without Wayne and Warren. I wish they were here to talk to."

"Your wish is my command," said the genie.

True or False?

1. Four men were shipwrecked.
2. Their ship sank in the Atlantic.
3. They built a hotel.
4. They thought they'd be rescued soon.
5. They left messages in the sand.
6. They sent messages by airmail.
7. Don found the bottle on the beach.
8. A genie jumped out of the bottle.
9. He gave the men three wishes.
10. All the men were sent home.

INTERVIEW

Rose Bush is an expert on plants and the environment. Our ESL Reporter is interviewing her at an experimental greenhouse.

ESL: I understand that many trees are dying.

B: That's right. There's a huge amount of pollution in the air. Pollution kills trees, plants, even animals.

ESL: Where does the pollution come from?

B: Well, some of it comes from factories. Some of it comes from cars and trucks.

ESL: How does pollution spread?

B: The wind carries it. It spreads it far away from the place where it began. When it rains, the pollution in the air comes back down. We call that acid rain.

ESL: Why is acid rain a bad thing?

B: Acid rain is killing whole forests. It's poisoning the soil. It's poisoning our lakes and rivers.

ESL: Is acid rain really a serious problem?

B: Absolutely. Some scientists believe that in twenty years all the great forests of the world may be dead.

Reading/role-playing an interview

1. Make a chart of traffic patterns in your town or city. First, list all the different vehicles you can think of. Then stand on a corner, and check off all the vehicles that pass in 15 minutes. Do this at different times on different days if you can. When was there the most traffic? When was there the least traffic? What kinds of pollution did you see?

2. Find out more about acid rain. Find out more about how we are getting rid of garbage . . . not just ordinary garbage, but dangerous garbage. This kind of garbage is called toxic waste.

3. Did you know that many things in your home can be dangerous to your health?

Products like oven cleaner, drain cleaner, paint, bug sprays—even furniture polish can be dangerous. You can find out more by writing to the Sierra Club. Your teacher has the address.

Dear Themework,
   A bunch of us made a chart on traffic patterns in front of our school. In the morning, the traffic was terrible. We counted 643 cars, trucks, and buses in just fifteen minutes! We were really busy. And the air was terrible. Now I know why the trees are dying.

   Yours truly,
   Frank Hogan

CALLA: Questioning for clarification

Social studies: pollution
Cooperative learning/research and report

Problem Solving

I'm a pilot. My name is Ed Eagle. I fly a helicopter. I work for the Coast Guard. When the weather is bad, I'm on alert for an emergency.

Last week, I was on patrol. The weather was foggy and cold. I knew that five ships were in port. I flew over the harbor. I could see five ships below. Every ship had two lights.

On the left, the lights were red, like this:

On the right, the lights were green, like this:

All the ships were moving slowly at about the same speed. I saw that two ships were going to crash. There was nothing I could do.

Which two ships crashed?

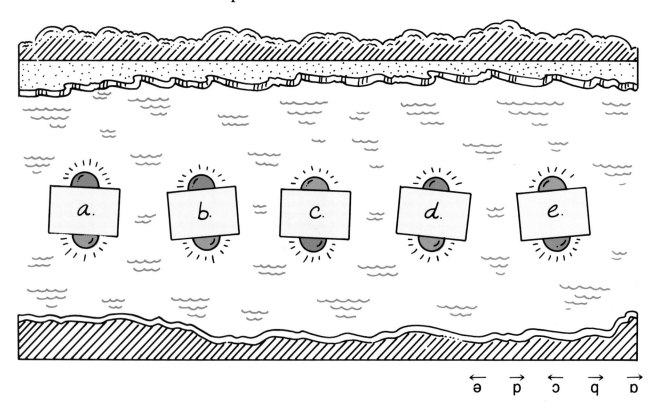

Ships C and D crashed. Only two ships were heading directly for each other. Red is left; green is right. The ships were moving like this:

76   Applying logic to solve problems

Bed in Summer

In winter I get up at night
And dress by yellow candlelight.
In summer, quite the other way,
I have to go to bed by day.

I have to go to bed and see
The birds still hopping on the trees,
Or hear the grown-up people's feet
Still going past me in the street.

And does it not seem hard to you,
When all the sky is clear and blue,
And I should like so much to play,
To have to go to bed by day?

Robert Louis Stevenson

Literature: poem
Rhythm and rhyme
Creative writing

77

Listening Comprehension

You are going to listen to the first part of a famous story. Listen carefully and complete the sentences below. Write your answers on a separate piece of paper.

1. The family was
   a. killed at sea.
   b. shipwrecked at sea.
   c. lost at sea.

2. The ship was half sunk
   a. on an island.
   b. on rocks near an island.
   c. on rocks far away from an island.

3. The family searched
   a. the ship.
   b. the rocks.
   c. the island.

4. They built a
   a. house.
   b. boat.
   c. hut.

5. On the island, they found food—
   a. coconuts and ice cream.
   b. pineapple and yogurt.
   c. coconuts and pineapple.

6. The man's wife found some
   a. huge, tall trees.
   b. huge, tall buildings.
   c. huge, tall animals.

Listening for information
Literature: Swiss Family Robinson
Multiple choice

You are going to read the next part of "Swiss Family Robinson." Read carefully and answer the questions below. Write your answers in full sentences on a separate piece of paper.

1. What did the family name the island?
2. How many people were in the family?
3. What animals did they tame?
4. What did they make candles from?
5. What did they put on the hill near the treehouse?
6. Why did they decide to blow up the wreck?

And so, we were safe and sound in our treehouse. We decided to name our island New Switzerland, after our homeland. Weeks and months passed. We discovered many things. My wife and my sons Fritz, Ernest, Jack and Francis spent many days exploring. We caught and tamed a wild buffalo and an eagle. My wife found some unusual berries. They were sticky. She put them in a pot and melted them. Then she made candles from the juice.

We kept taking things from the wreck. We found two small cannons. We floated them to shore. We put them on a hill to protect our treehouse.

After some months, there was nothing left on the wreck of our ship. We decided to blow it up. We hoped the wood from the ship would float ashore. My sons and I rolled a barrel of gunpowder into the bottom of the ship. We made a very long fuse. We lit it and left the ship. We got back to our island. There was a huge explosion. The wreck was gone.

What do you think happened next? Make up your own ending.

The Something

Excerpted from the book by Natalie Babbitt

The truth is that Mylo was very much afraid of the dark.
When his mother asked him why, he had a hard time
answering.

Finally he said, "I keep thinking something will come in
through the window."

"What kind of a something?" asked Mylo's mother.
"Robbers, I suppose? Or ghosts? There's no such thing as
ghosts, you know. And even if we had some robbers, they
wouldn't be interested in you."

♫♪
📼 Literature: contemporary classic
Shared reading

"I'm not worried about robbers," said Mylo.

"Well, what is it, then?" said Mylo's mother.

"Just a Something," said Mylo.

His mother felt very bad about not being able to help him. So the next day she went out and bought a large package of modeling clay and gave it to him and that made her feel better.

Mylo didn't know what to do with the clay at first. Mostly he made lumps and thumb prints. Or rolled it into snakes.

But after a while he found himself trying to make a statue of the Something he was afraid of in the night.

Every day he worked with the clay. And every day he learned a little more about how to make it do what he wanted.

He was trying to figure out exactly what the Something looked like. He found himself almost wishing it WOULD come in through the window so he could get a good look at it and make a better statue in the morning.

Then one day everything seemed to go just right, and suddenly there it was. He had made a perfect statue of the Something. He was very proud of his work.

When he showed it to his mother, she said, "That's beautiful, Mylo," in such a special voice that he knew she had no idea what it was.

But it didn't matter. Mylo didn't try to explain. He carried the statue to his room and put it on the table by his bed.

That night Mylo went right to sleep and dreamed he was wandering out in the wild dark. He came to a sort of window, and all at once, the Something was there, climbing through.

It was the very Something he had modeled out of clay. But he found he wasn't afraid any more.

He spoke right up to it. "Hello," he said. "My name is Mylo and I'm not afraid of you at all."

"I'm not afraid of you either," said the Something. "But I wish you'd get out of my dream."

"This isn't your dream," said Mylo. "This is my dream. And anyway, I was just leaving."

"Goodbye then," said the Something. "It was nice talking to you."

Literature: contemporary classic

And then Mylo woke up.

In the morning his mother said, "Aren't you going to play with your clay today?"

"No," said Mylo. "I'm tired of it now."

But he kept the statue of the Something for a long time afterward. He kept it because he was the only one who knew what it was. And he didn't want to forget too quickly.

Sally and Phil Links own the Links Bicycle Factory. Sally and Phil employ five people.

1. It's a small business, so sometimes, people do more than one job. But usually, Sally assembles the frames.

2. Pedro Verde paints the frames. Sometimes he paints them red. Sometimes he paints them blue.

3. The frames go to the factory floor.

4. Phil Links adds the handlebars and the wheels.

Social studies: community life
Describing people/places/actions
Reading for information

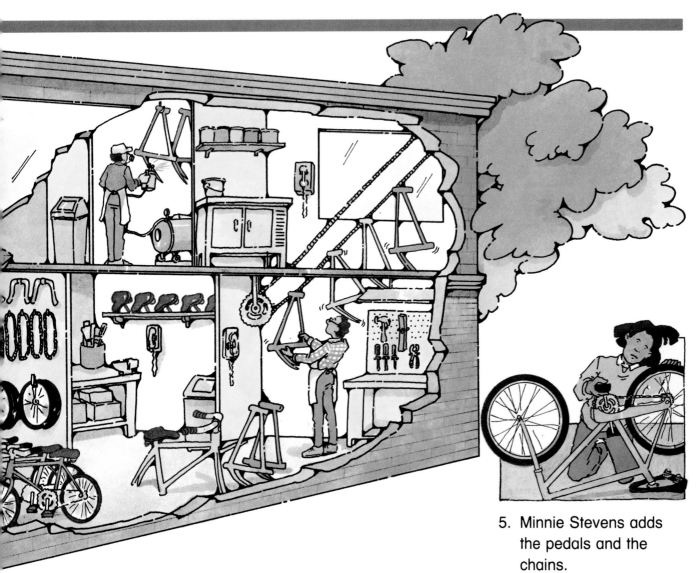

5. Minnie Stevens adds
   the pedals and the
   chains.

6. Nak Choung adds the
   brakes and the lights.

7. Ann Strunk test rides
   each bike. She makes
   sure that each bike is
   well-made.

8. Sally and Phil are going
   to open a store in the
   new mall. Their son Mike
   is going to run the store.
   He will also repair bikes.

♪♪ Social studies: community life
Describing people/places/actions
📼 Reading for imformation
87

🎵🎵 Making plans
Role-playing fixed and free dialogues
Creating new dialogues from cues

Say the right thing!

Can I help you?
Have you still got tickets
to the game?

Yes, three tickets for the play,
please.
Yes, a few at $15.00 a seat.

$15.00! That's expensive.
For which day?

Tuesday.
Yes, but it's an important game.

Afternoon or evening?
Well, do you have three together?

Yes. That'll be $45.00.
Evening, please.

How many seats?
Here you are—$45.00

Four. Three children, one adult.
Enjoy the game.

Now make conversations with your partner. Begin with these situations.

1. You want to go to the Whale Show. Buy tickets for two children and two adults. Buy the tickets for Wednesday night.

2. You want to go to the play. Buy tickets for one child and one adult. Buy the tickets for Saturday night.

♪♫ Role-playing fixed dialogues
Understanding sequence in conversations
Creating new dialogues from cues

89

Pair Practice 1

Consonant plus y = ied	Vowel plus y = yed	Double consonants
try-tried	play-played	stop-stopped
cry-cried	enjoy-enjoyed	step-stepped
dry-dried	stay-stayed	beg-begged
hurry-hurried	employ-employed	jog-jogged
carry-carried		rip-ripped

*Look at the pictures. Work with your partner. Take turns
asking and answering these questions.*

1. Who did the clown marry?

2. What did the dog bury?

3. What did the girl dry?

4. What did he play?

5. What did they enjoy?

6. Where did they stop?

Understanding verb forms
Asking for/giving information
Spelling regular verb endings

Mrs. Vink and her son Max were leaving on vacation. She packed her suitcase. He packed his suitcase. Then he carried the bags to the front door. Mrs. Vink opened the front door and walked outside. Max went to call a taxi.

First he checked the living room. He didn't want to forget anything. He noticed some books. He picked them up and slipped them into his suitcase. Then Max checked the kitchen. The coffee pot wasn't turned off. He turned it off. Then Max checked the back door. It wasn't locked. He locked it. He checked the bedroom too. The window was open. He closed it. He checked the bathroom. The shower was dripping. He stepped into the tub. He turned the shower the wrong way. Cold water sprayed all over him. He changed his clothes. He dried his hair. Finally, he hurried out the front door.

"What *have* you been doing?" Mrs. Vink demanded. "And where is that taxi you called?"

"Taxi? Oh, gosh. I *forgot* the taxi!"

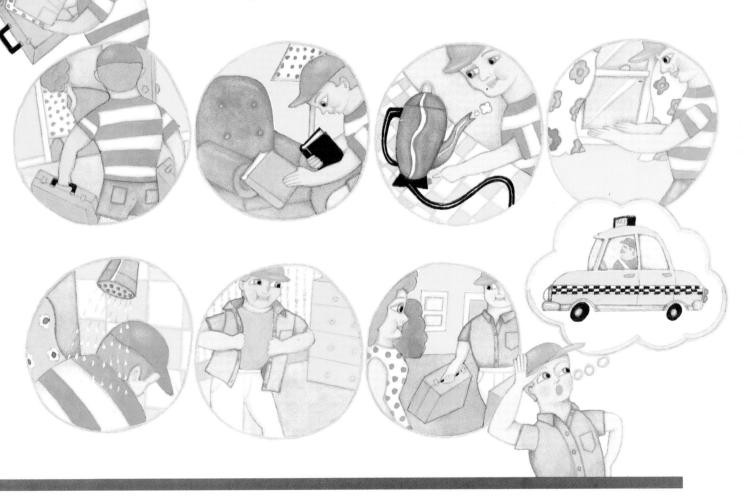

Study Skills

Skim the article to decide whether the statements are true or false. Rewrite all the false statements on a separate piece of paper.

1. The Antarctic is the region around the North Pole.
2. The Arctic is one of the two polar regions.
3. The Arctic is hot in summer.
4. Mukluks are boats made of skins.

5. The native people came from Asia.
6. The Bering Strait is an island.
7. All villages have schools.
8. A kayak is a kind of boat.

· ·

Life in the Arctic

The two coldest places in the world are the Arctic, the area around the North Pole, and the Antarctic, the area around the South Pole. They are called the polar regions.

In the Arctic winter, temperatures can drop as low as −60! Even in summer, it doesn't get very hot. Sometimes there is snow in summer. The ground is always frozen beneath the surface. This frozen area is called permafrost.

The native people of the Arctic are usually called Eskimos. They came from Asia thousands of years ago. Find the body of water called the Bering Strait on a map. It is only 56 miles wide. People could have walked across the strait when it was frozen. There might also have been a land bridge where the strait now is.

Many of the natives of Alaska still wear fur clothing. They dress in layers, and wear mukluks—fur boots.

Travel in the Arctic is a mixture of the old and new. People still use dog sleds and kayaks, but they also use snowmobiles and motorboats. Small planes also fly regularly between many places in the Arctic.

Reading for information/research
Social studies: geography
True/false statements

CALLA: Imagery

Until recently, all Eskimo men were hunters and fishermen. That was the way they got their food, and the way they got skins for clothing, blankets, and boats. Today, they buy most things from stores or mail-order catalogues. Men run small stores, work on the Alaskan pipe line, carve and paint beautiful pieces of art, and act as guides for Arctic travelers.

Only the largest villages have schools. Children from the small villages go to regional schools. They live together during the school year. Then they go back to their families when the school term is over.

Favorite sports are ice hockey and sledding.

Eskimos don't really live in igloos. Most homes are built of stone or wood. There's plenty of rock in the Arctic, but wood is scarce. Because it is scarce, wood is expensive.

Life is changing fast in the Arctic.

Pair Practice 2

take(s)	took	taken	break(s)	broke	broken
fall(s)	fell	fallen	tear(s)	tore	torn
throw(s)	threw	thrown	begin(s)	began	begun
know(s)	knew	known	swim(s)	swam	swum
go(es)	went	gone	see(s)	saw	seen

Take turns with your partner. Read the sentences aloud and choose the right form of the verb.

1. ★ I (go, went) to the movies yesterday.
   ● What did you (saw, see)?
   ★ I (see, saw) *Snow White*.
   ● Oh, I have already (saw, seen) it.

2. ★ Did you (went, go) to the beach
     last weekend?
   ● Yes, I (swim, swam) in the ocean.
     Then I (fell, fall) on some rocks,
     and I (tore, tear) my bathing suit.

3. ★ Janet (takes, took) the bus every day.
   ● Where does she (go, went)?
   ★ She (went, goes) to work downtown.

4. ★ I (take, took) a math test yesterday.
   ● Did you (knew, know) everything?
   ★ Of course not!

5. ★ Have you (saw, seen) my newspaper?
   ● I (threw, throw) it away.
   ★ But why?
   ● The dog (torn, tore) it up.

♪♫
Understanding verb forms
Role-playing fixed and free dialogues

Mike and Bob went to the movies. It was a western. Outlaws had taken over a town.

The sheriff knew he needed help. He called a U.S. Marshal. "Come as fast as you can," the sheriff said. The U.S. Marshal began the long trip.

The outlaws were waiting for the marshal. They were hiding by the river. "I'll bet the marshal falls off his horse," said Mike.

"Nonsense," replied Bob. "He's the hero. I'll bet you he *doesn't* fall off." The two friends sat in silence for a few more minutes.

The marshal came to the river. The outlaws jumped out of their hiding place. The marshal's horse tripped, and threw the marshal into the river. The marshal swam to shore and took cover behind a rock.

"I told you so!" Mike said.

"I can't believe it," Bob replied.

"Well, I have something to tell you," Mike said. "I have seen this movie before. I knew what was going to happen."

"Well, I have seen this movie before, too!" Bob said. "But I didn't think the marshal would be so stupid and fall off his horse again!"

INTERVIEW

Adam King has a very unusual job. He is the falconer at an Air Force Base. A falconer trains falcons to hunt for other birds. Our ESL Reporter is interviewing him.

ESL: Why does the Air Force need a falconer?

K: Because of bird strikes. That's when a large flock of birds fly into an airplane. A bird strike can damage engines. It's like throwing a rock at a car that's going over 100 miles per hour.

ESL: But are bird strikes common?

K: Yes. Over 1,000 bird strikes at airports have been reported this year.

ESL: Why do birds like airports?

K: Well, there is plenty of food in the open fields around an airport. And in the summer, after a heavy rain, thousands of worms crawl out onto the runways.

ESL: Do the falcons kill the other birds?

K: No, we don't train them to kill. We train them to chase the other birds away.

ESL: How do you train your falcons?

K: Falcons will only do their job for food. After every flight, the falcon gets a mouse.

ESL: How high do the falcons fly?

K: They patrol from about 3,000 feet. They can see any birds that try to fly over the airport.

ESL: And how fast do the falcons fly?

K: In a dive, falcons can reach speeds of 120 miles per hour. It takes years to train a falcon. You can get very fond of them.

Reading/role-playing an interview
Science: biology

Themework Teamwork

1. Think about how animals help us. Make a chart with these headings:

Work	Clothing	Food	Entertainment

Find out which animals belong in each list. Some may go under more than one heading. We eat the meat of sheep, for example. We also use their wool for clothing. Horses work on farms; they also entertain us in races, the circus, etc.

2. Make another chart with these headings:

Wild	Tame	Extinct

Find out which animals belong in each list. Then choose one animal for a special report. Find out all you can about the animal. Organize your information for an oral report. Show pictures or make drawings.

3. Do you have a pet? Tell about it. Have you trained your pet to do any special tricks? If you don't have a pet, write and tell about a pet you'd like to have.

Dear Themework,
    I had a dog, but it died. For a long time, I was lonely for a pet. Then my dad took me to the Animal Shelter. I found the cutest puppy. He is gray now, but when he was a puppy, he was black. I trained him to take food only from my left hand. I trained him to roll over, to sit up, and to "wave" hello. My dog was a Christmas present, so I named him Chris Kringle.

Yours,
Kathy Sands

Read and Do

How to Make Magnetic Sailboats

You need: A plastic tray, a magnet, some pins, tape, a ruler,
paper, and a thin sheet of foam or cork.

1. Cut some boat shapes from the foam or cork.

2. Push three or four pins horizontally into each boat.

3. Push one pin vertically into each. This is the mast.

4. Cut out paper sails and tape them to the masts.

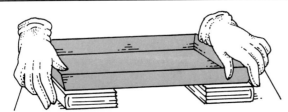

5. Place the tray on two boxes or piles of books with space underneath.

6. Tape the magnet to the ruler. Pour some water into the tray. Make some islands if you like.

7. Move the magnet under the tray. With practice, you'll be able to steer around the islands. Perhaps you can have some races with your friends.

The Dog and the Bone

One day, a dog was out taking a walk. He was carrying a bone in his mouth. As he was walking across a bridge, he looked down at the river.

The dog saw his own reflection in the water. But he thought it was another dog. "There's a dog looking up at me," he thought. "And he has a bone, too. That bone looks bigger than my bone. I'll frighten that dog and grab his bone away."

The dog began to bark. And, of course, as soon as he opened his mouth, he dropped his bone. It fell into the river and floated away. The dog had been very silly.

Don't be greedy for what others have.

Listening Comprehension

You are going to listen to some information about sharks. Listen carefully and complete the sentences below. Write your answers on a separate piece of paper.

1. Which is true?
   a. All sharks are dangerous.
   b. Some sharks are dangerous.
   c. Most sharks are dangerous.

2. Attacks on humans by the great white shark
   a. are rare.
   b. don't happen.
   c. are common.

3. Sharks are
   a. blind.
   b. deaf.
   c. color-blind.

4. Sharks live an average of
   a. 20 years.
   b. 10 years.
   c. 70 years.

5. Sharks can smell blood up to
   a. a mile away.
   b. a quarter of a mile away.
   c. two miles away.

Listening for information: factual article
Multiple choice

Reading Comprehension

You are going to read some information about sharks. Read carefully and decide whether the statements below are true or false. Write your answers on a separate piece of paper. Rewrite the false sentences so that they are true.

1. There are more than 400 kinds of sharks.
2. Sharks have 24,000 bones in their bodies.
3. The skin of sharks is smooth.
4. The teeth of sharks are razor-sharp.
5. The smallest shark is only about 12 inches long.
6. The largest shark can be 720 inches long.
7. Sharks are slow in the water.
8. The carpet shark has a clever disguise.

If you have seen any of the *Jaws* movies, you may think all sharks are dangerous to humans. Well, they're not. There are more than 300 species of sharks. Only the blue pointer, the zembesi, tiger, mako, hammerhead, and grey nurse sharks have been known to eat humans.

Except for its jaws, a shark has no bones in its body. Its skeleton is made of cartilage. Its skin is rough, like sandpaper. Most sharks have around 24,000 razor-sharp teeth!

The smallest species of shark is the dwarf shark. It is only a foot long. The largest species of shark is the whale shark. It can reach 60 feet in length and weigh up to 13 tons.

Sharks are fast swimmers. They can reach speeds of 50 miles per hour. Perhaps the strangest shark is the wobbegong, or carpet shark. It has a spotted head with a fringe. This is a clever disguise, and the shark is able to sneak up on its prey.

The Land I Lost

Excerpted from the book by Huynh Quang Nhuong

I was born in the central highlands of Vietnam. Our small hamlet was on a riverbank that had a deep jungle on one side and a chain of high mountains on the other. Across the river, rice fields stretched to the slopes of another chain of mountains.

There were fifty houses in our hamlet. The houses were made of bamboo and covered with coconut leaves. Each was surrounded by a deep trench to protect it from wild animals or thieves. The only way to enter a house was to walk across a "monkey bridge." That was a single, bamboo stick. At night, we pulled the bridges into our houses and were safe.

 Literature: contemporary autobiography
Shared reading
Creative writing

There were no shops or marketplaces in our hamlet. If we needed supplies—medicine, cloth, soap, candles—we had to cross over the mountains to a town nearby.

During the six-month rainy season, nearly all of us helped plant and cultivate crops. We grew rice, sweet potatoes, Indian mustard, eggplant, tomatoes, hot pepper, and corn. During the dry season, we became hunters and turned to the jungle. Wild animals played a very large part in our lives. There were four animals we feared most: the tiger, the wild hog, the crocodile, and the horse snake.

Like all farmers' children, I started working at the age of six. My seven sisters helped by working in the kitchen, gathering eggs, or taking water to the cattle. I looked after our herd of water buffaloes. I fished for the family, too.

My father was a farmer and a hunter, but he had a college education. In the evenings, he helped to teach other children in the hamlet. It was too small to afford a professional teacher.

My mother managed the house. During the harvest season, she could be found in the fields, helping my father. As the wife of a hunter, she knew how to dress and nurse a wound. She took good care of her husband and his hunting dogs.

I went to the lowlands to study for a while. I wanted to follow my father as a teacher when I grew up. I always planned to return to my hamlet to live the rest of my life there. But war disrupted my dreams. The land I love was lost to me forever.

The *Sunnyville News* is
published once a week.

1. Warren Stones is the editor of the
news section. He knows everything
about local and world events.

2. Sandy Score is the editor of the
sports section. She knows
everything about sports and sports
stars.

3. Harriet Rock is the editor of the
entertainment section. She knows
everything about music, movies,
plays, and TV.

Social studies: community life
Identifying and describing people/places/actions
Reading for information

4. Clara Bows is the editor of the fashion and food section. She knows everything about cooking and clothes.

5. Freddy Add is the editor of the classified section. He knows everything about buying and selling things.

6. Bob Job is the editor of the employment section. He knows everything about jobs and business.

7. The reporters write the stories.
8. The editors check the stories.

9. The layout crew makes up the pages.

10. The pressmen print the newspapers.

11. The truck drivers deliver the newspapers.

♪♪ Social studies: community life
Identifying and describing people/places/actions
Reading for information

107

DATA BANK

small	petite	ugly	too small
medium	average	beautiful	too big
large	long	pretty	too long
extra-large	extra-long	neat	too short

Shopping
Role-playing fixed and free dialogues
Creating new dialogues from cues

Say the right thing!

Can I help you?
Something for you today?

Yes, I'd like a sweater.
Yes, I need a birthday present.

For a boy or a girl?
What size?

A girl.
I wear medium.

Any particular color?
How about one of these scarves?

Blue, if you have it.
How much are they?

They're $25.00.
Here's a nice blue one.

How much is it?
What? $25.00! That's too much!

It's $12.00.
Well, these are on sale for $8.00.

Fine. I'll take it.
That's better. I'll take a pink one.

Now make conversations with your partner.
Begin with these situations.

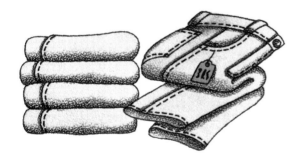

1. You are shopping for yourself.
   You want a new pair of jeans.
   Tell the clerk what size you wear.
   Tell the clerk what color you want.
   Ask the price.
   Will you buy the jeans or not?

2. You are shopping for a present.
   Your friend is a boy.
   You see a neat record.
   You ask how much it is.
   It's too expensive.
   What do you buy instead?

Role-playing fixed dialogues
Understanding sequence in conversation
Creating new dialogues from cues

109

Pair Practice 1

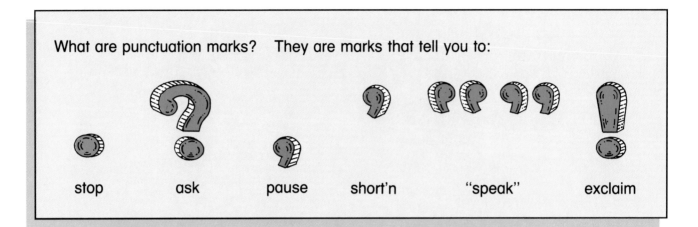

What are punctuation marks?   They are marks that tell you to:

stop   ask   pause   short'n   "speak"   exclaim

1. the PERIOD   • :

   When you come to the end of a
   thought,
   Sign off with this dot.

2. the QUESTION MARK ? :

   At the end of something you
   must ask,
   Making this mark is your task.

3. the COMMA , :

   A sentence is a band of words
   going for a walk.
   A comma is a pause for breath
   when you talk.
   And when you write,
   you use the comma because
   it gives your reader a
   chance to pause.

4. the APOSTROPHE ' :

   An apostrophe shows who
   owns a thing,

   Like *Mary's* hat, my *sister's* cat,
   and a *girl's* ring.
   An apostrophe also shrinks
   words—*do not* into *don't,
   Have not* to *haven't* and *will
   not* to *won't.*

5. QUOTATION MARKS " " :

   They let you know who says
   what,
   A pair of marks is what you've
   got.
   "Wow!" said Ben.
   "What?" asked Tim.
   "No," replied Sally.

6. EXCLAMATION MARK ! :

   If you want to scare, command,
   or excite,
   It's the mark that you should
   write.

The Pirate Flag

Take turns reading the following story out loud with a partner. One of you should read the words. The other should read the punctuation marks. How? Just follow the simple code at the bottom of the page.

"What ho!" cried Pirate Pat, sitting in the crow's nest. "Thunder and lightning! There's a treasure ship. Look lively, my cutthroats!"

Pirate Pat slid down to the ship's deck.

"How far away is the ship?" asked Blackbeard, the pirate captain.

"We'll meet the ship before the sun sets," said Pirate Pat. "What are your orders, Captain?"

"Mates! Listen!" called Blackbeard. "Put up a false flag. Stay well hidden. When we're almost upon them, we'll raise our flag. Raise the pirate flag! That'll be a beautiful surprise, hey?" And Blackbeard laughed a deep, mean, nasty, chilling, scary, gruesome, eerie, wild, awful, terrifying, pirate laugh.

.	**Bong**
"	**Beep**
?	**Ding**
,	**Hummm**
!	**Boing**
'	**Poof**

Study Skills

Skim the articles to decide whether the statments are true or false. Rewrite all the false statements on a separate piece of paper.

1. A rain forest is hot and wet.
2. Average rainfall is twice the amount that New York City gets.
3. Amazon houses are full of light.
4. The Indians raise corn and pigs.
5. Girls learn how to hunt and fish.
6. Amazon houses look like haystacks.
7. The Indians wear heavy clothing.
8. The Amazon Indians are not related to Indians in other parts of the world.

▪ ▪

Life in the Rain Forest

Find the Amazon River on a map of Brazil. The land surrounding the river is a huge rain forest. The Amazon rain forest is very hot and rainy. The trees grow tall and close together. It rains an average of 100 inches a year. That's twice the rainfall of New York City. There is always rain falling somewhere in the Amazon rain forest.

The Amazon Indians are distant relatives of Indians of North America. Their ancestors crossed the Bering Strait thousands of years ago. The Amazon Indians have darker skin and shorter bodies than North American Indians. Most of these Indians have the same way of life as their ancestors.

Amazon Indians build houses that look like haystacks. They use dried palm leaves or grasses for the roof and walls. Some Indians make their walls from thin tree trunks or mud.

Reading for information/research
Social studies: geography
True/false statements

CALLA:
Selective
attention

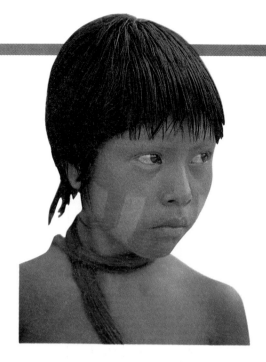

Each house has one big room. There are no windows. The floor is dirt. Parents, children, grandparents, aunts and uncles live together. Sometimes as many as 70 people live in one house.

The Indians of the rain forest wear little or no clothing. They don't need to stay warm. On special occasions, these Indians paint their bodies with beautiful colors and designs.

These Indians farm some fruits and vegetables. Corn and cassava are the most important crops. The Indians are very skillful hunters. They use spears, blowguns, and bows and arrows. They hunt wild pigs, monkeys, turtles, and many kinds of fish.

Children go to school, but not to learn reading, writing, or arithmetic.

Girls learn how to search for honey and fruit, plant crops, weave, and care for younger children. Boys learn how to hunt and fish.

Life is changing fast in the Amazon, however. The forests are being cleared. Roads and towns are being built. The old ways are being replaced by "modern" life.

Pair Practice 2

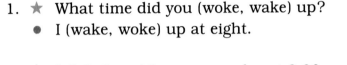

wake(s)	woke	woken	go(es)	went	gone
grow(s)	grew	grown	see(s)	saw	seen
shake(s)	shook	shaken	speak(s)	spoke	spoken
drink(s)	drank	drunk	eat(s)	ate	eaten

Work with your partner. Take turns asking and answering the questions.

1. ★ What time did you (woke, wake) up?
   ● I (wake, woke) up at eight.

2. ★ I (left, leave) home every day at 8:00.
   ● Did you (left, leave) yesterday at 8:00?
   ★ No, I (leaves, left) at 9:00 yesterday.
   ● Where did you (went, go)?
   ★ I (go, went) to the museum.

3. ★ Lou (wake, wakes) up every day at 6:00.
   ● Where does he (went, go) first?
   ★ He (gone, goes) to the kitchen.

4. ★ Have you ever (ate, eaten) snake?
   ● No, but I have (eat, eaten) octopus!

5. ★ Last year, we (grow, grew) tomatoes.
   We (eaten, ate) tomatoes every day.
   We (drunk, drank) tomato juice
   every day.
   We have all (grew, grown) tired of
   tomatoes.

Understanding verb forms
Choosing correct verb forms in context

Lou woke up. He looked at the clock, turned over, and went back to sleep. The alarm woke him up again. Still he didn't get up.

Lou's mother saw her son still asleep in bed. She shook him by the shoulders. "Come on, Lou. Time to get ready for school."

"I don't want to go!" Lou said. "I can't stand the thought of school."

"Now, Lou. We both know you have to go. I have grown tired of telling you that every day. Now, get up!" Lou finally got up.

Later, after Lou had eaten his breakfast, his mother spoke to him again. "You'll be late, Lou. Have you seen what time it is?"

"I don't care if I'm late. I don't care if I never go to school again!"

"Son, you know as well as I do—you have to go."

"Give me two good reasons," Lou said.

"First, you are forty-two years old. And second, you're the principal!"

INTERVIEW

Anna Walker works at a large zoo. She is an expert on animals. Her favorite animal is the koala bear. Our ESL Reporter is interviewing her.

ESL: Tell us about koala bears, Anna.

W: They're short, fat little animals. They come from Australia. They look like toy bears.

ESL: But they're not bears, are they?

W: No, they're not. They're marsupials. Marsupials are animals with pouches. When a baby koala is born, it's no bigger than a bee. It has no hair, and it can't see. But it makes its way into the mother's pouch. If a baby doesn't find its way into the pouch, it dies.

ESL: How long does the baby stay inside the pouch?

W: From a few weeks up to six months.

ESL: What happens when the baby koala leaves the pouch?

W: After that, the baby likes to ride on its mother's back. Koalas live in Eucalyptus trees. They sleep all day and eat at night. They eat about a pound of leaves every night!

ESL: Are there many marsupials in the world?

W: No, not many. Most of them like koalas and kangaroos live in or near Australia.

ESL: Do people hunt koalas?

W: Not any more. It's against the law, now.

ESL: Good!

Reading/role-playing an interview

1. You have read about many animals in this book. Go back through the book and make a list. Add animals you want to know more about to the list. Concentrate on the babies. Write down everything you find out about how they are born, what their first months are like, what their mothers and fathers do, etc.

2. Share your information with a partner. Choose your favorite baby animals for poster displays. Organize your information for oral reports.

3. Work with several friends to make quiz cards. Write questions on the front of each card. Write answers on the back. Then play "Animal Quiz" in teams. Play with other classes. Who knows the most about animals?

> Koalas
> 1. Are koalas bears?
> 2. How big is a new-born?
> 3. Can it see?

> Koalas
> 1. No, they're marsupials.
> 2. It's no bigger than a bee.
> 3. No, it can't.

Dear Themework,
    I really liked the last project. I liked looking back in the book. I had forgotten a lot of facts about animals. My friends and I have written over 50 quiz cards so far. We have played two games of "Animal Quiz" with other classes. We won both games! It felt great to know the most answers!

Best,
Shirley Hassim

♪♪ Social studies (animal life)
🔊 Cooperative learning/research and report
Socializing/turn-taking

Problem Solving

There's going to be a road race next month. Here's the map. As a runner, you can follow either the roads or the paths. The roads are the black lines. The paths are the dotted lines.

You will start at A and finish at G. You must pass through Checkpoint C, but you can take any route you want after that. Find the fastest route! Be careful. One mile by path takes the same time as five miles by road.

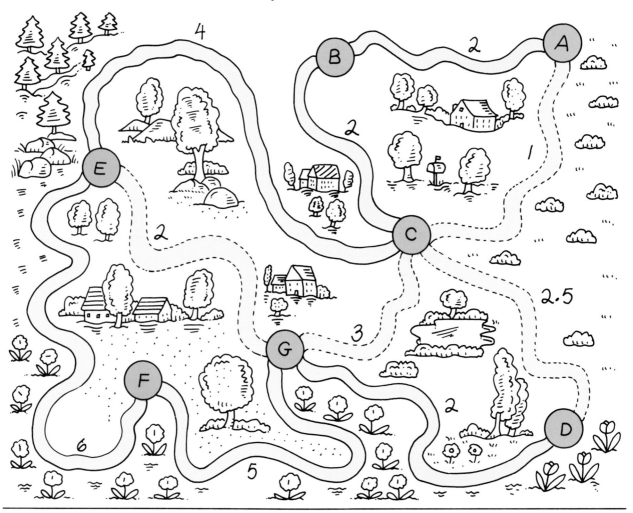

A – B – C – E – G = 18 miles by road. From A to C, the road (4 miles) is shorter than the path (equivalent to 5 miles).

C – E – F – G   4 + 6 + 5 = 15
C – G   3 × 5 = 15
C – D – G   (2.5 × 5) + 2 = 14.5
C – E – G   4 + (2 × 5) = 14

Ears Hear

Flies buzz,
Motors roar.
Kettles hiss,
People snore.
Dogs bark,
Birds cheep.
Autos honk: Beep! Beep!

Winds sigh,
Shoes squeak.
Trucks honk,
Floors creak.
Whistles toot,
Bells clang.
Doors slam: Bang! Bang!

Kids shout,
Clocks ding.
Babies cry,
Phones ring.
Balls bounce,
Spoons drop.
People scream: Stop! Stop!

Lucia and James L. Hymes, Jr.

Listening Comprehension

You are going to listen to the first part of a famous story. Listen carefully and take notes. Then answer the questions below in complete sentences. Write your answers on a separate piece of paper.

1. Who was working hard?
2. What time of year was it?
3. Did his head ache, or did his back ache?
4. What two things were calling to him?
5. Did he cross the road or some fields?
6. What had he never seen before?
7. Where did he sit?
8. Where did he see the Water Rat?
9. How did the Water Rat get across the river?
10. Where did the two animals agree to go?

♫♪ Listening for information
Literature: Wind in the Willows
Answering information questions

Reading Comprehension

You are going to read the next part of "The Wind in the Willows." Read carefully and decide whether the sentences below are true or false. Rewrite the false sentences so that they are true. Write your answers on a separate piece of paper.

1. The Water Rat fetched a paper bag.
2. Mole settled back on the soft cushions.
3. Ratty rowed and talked loudly.
4. They met the Otter and the Turtle.
5. Toad shot by on a bicycle.
6. Toad was short and fat.
7. Toad soon grows tired of things.
8. Toad had an airplane last year.
9. Mole and Rat went back to Mole's house.
10. Mole went to sleep in a comfy bedroom.

The Water Rat fetched a wicker picnic basket. "Shove that under your feet," he said to the Mole. The Mole settled back on the soft cushions, and Ratty rowed silently down the river. Mole took in all the new sights, smells and sounds of the river. Soon they came to a nice place for their picnic.

While they were eating, they met two of Ratty's friends—the Otter and the Badger. Mr. Toad was on the river, too. He shot by in a new racing boat. He was short and fat, splashing badly, and rolling from side to side. "Toad's always trying something new," explained Rat. "Last year, he had a houseboat. But he soon gets tired of things."

The Rat and the Mole went back to Rat's snug home in the River Bank. They sat in armchairs beside a bright fire, chatting away. Rat invited Mole to stay with him for the summer. The happy Mole went to sleep in a comfy bedroom. His new friend, the River, was lapping against the bank. And he could hear the wind, whispering in the willows.

Rat and Mole have a very happy summer together. Make up some adventures for them. Include Mr. Toad, too.

Reading for information/predicting/creative writing
Literature: Wind in the Willows
True/false statements

121

Alexander and the Terrible, Horrible, No Good, Very Bad Day

From the book by Judith Viorst

I went to sleep with gum in my mouth and now there's gum in my hair and when I got out of bed this morning I tripped on the skateboard and by mistake I dropped my sweater in the sink while the water was running and I could tell it was going to be a terrible, horrible, no good, very bad day.

♪♪ Literature: contemporary classic
Shared reading
Creative writing

At breakfast Anthony found a Corvette Sting Ray car kit in his breakfast cereal box and Nick found a Junior Undercover Agent code ring in his breakfast cereal box but in my breakfast cereal box all I found was breakfast cereal.

I think I'll move to Australia.

In the car pool Mrs. Gibson let Becky have a seat by the window. Audry and Elliott got seats by the window too. I said I was being scrunched. I said I was being smushed. I said, if I don't get a seat by the window I am going to be carsick. No one even answered.

I could tell it was going to be a terrible, horrible, no good, very bad day.

At school Mrs. Dickens liked Paul's picture of the sailboat better than my picture of the invisible castle.

At singing time she said I sang too loud. At counting time she said I left out sixteen. Who needs sixteen?

I could tell it was going to be a terrible, horrible, no good, very bad day.

I could tell because Paul said I wasn't his best friend anymore. He said that Philip Parker was his best friend and that Albert Moyo was his next best friend and that I was only his third best friend.

I hope you sit on a tack, I said to Paul. I hope the next time you get a double-decker strawberry ice-cream cone the ice cream part falls off the cone part and lands in Australia.

Literature: contemporary classic

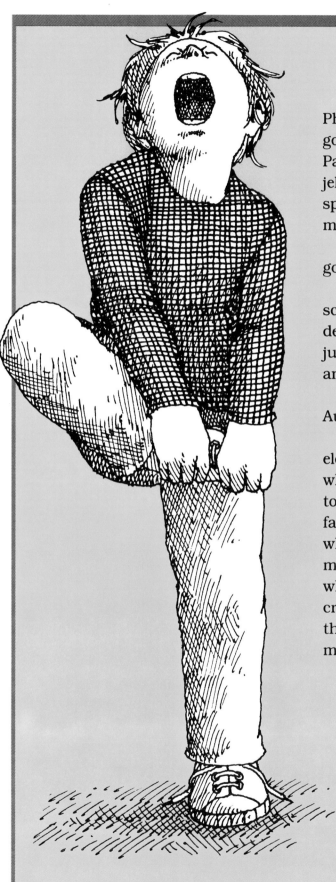

There were two cupcakes in Philip Parker's lunch bag and Albert got a Hershey bar with almonds and Paul's mother gave him a piece of jelly roll that had little coconut sprinkles on the top. Guess whose mother forgot to put in dessert?

It was a terrible, horrible, no good, very bad day.

That's what it was, because after school my mom took us all to the dentist and Dr. Fields found a cavity just in me. Come back next week and I'll fix it, said Dr. Fields.

Next week, I said, I'm going to Australia.

On the way downstairs the elevator door closed on my foot and while we were waiting for my mom to go get the car Anthony made me fall where it was muddy and then when I started crying because of the mud Nick said I was a crybaby and while I was punching Nick for saying crybaby my mom came back with the car and scolded me for being muddy and fighting.

I am having a terrible, horrible, no good, very bad day, I told everybody. No one even answered.

So then we went to the shoestore to buy some sneakers. Anthony chose white ones with blue stripes. Nick chose red ones with white stripes. I chose blue ones with red stripes but then the shoe man said, "We're all sold out." They made me buy plain old white ones, but they can't make me wear them.

Literature: contemporary classic

When we picked up my dad at his office he said I couldn't play with his copying machine, but I forgot. He also said to watch out for the books on his desk, and I was careful as could be except for my elbow. He also said don't fool around with his phone, but I think I called Australia. My dad said please don't pick him up anymore.

It was a terrible, horrible, no good, very bad day.

There were lima beans for dinner and I hate limas.

There was kissing on TV and I hate kissing.

My bath was too hot, I got soap in my eyes, my marble went down the drain, and I had to wear my railroad-train pajamas. I hate my railroad-train pajamas.

When I went to bed Nick took back the pillow he said I could keep and the Mickey Mouse night-light burned out and I bit my tongue.

The cat wants to sleep with Anthony, not with me. It has been a terrible, horrible, no good, very bad day. My mom says some days are like that.

Even in Australia.

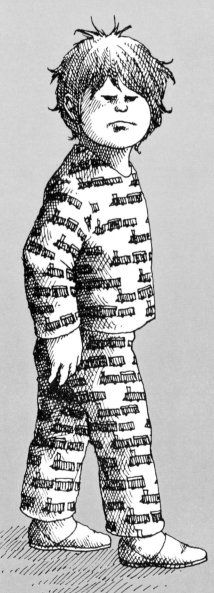

Skills Index

Note: For a comprehensive list of all skills covered in this level, see the Scope and Sequence Chart in the Teacher's Edition.

Linguistic Skills

Structures
adjectives: comparative/ superlative 28
adverbs: frequency 52–53
do forms 33, 114
how many 68
nouns: regular/irregular plurals 68
prepositions of place 46–47
pronouns 12–13
there is/are, was/were 46, 68

Verbs
habitual simple present tense
    regular 8, 32–33, 72, 114
    irregular 33, 114
simple past tense
    regular 64–65, 72–73, 90–91, 114
    irregular 32, 72, 94, 98, 114–115
present progressive tense 24–25
present perfect tense 52–53, 94–95, 114
modals
    can't, couldn't 49
    have to/has to, had to, will have to 48–49

Oral Communication
asking for/giving directions 46–47
asking for/giving information (throughout)
creating new dialogues from cues 6–7, 24, 49, 53, 67
describing
    actions, people, scenes 4–5, 24–25, 44–45, 64–65, 86–87, 106–107
    climate, environment 74–75, 92–93
    habitual actions 5, 8–9, 10–11, 33
    health 6–7, 64
    location 46–47
    ongoing actions 24–25
    past actions 32, 53, 64–65, 94
    physical characteristics 52–53
    planned future actions 48–49
    transportation 10–11, 75
discussing moral values 57, 99
expressing
    comparisons, contrasts 28–29, 92–93, 108–109
    greetings, leave-takings 6–7
    inability 49
    likes, dislikes 8–9, 27, 28–29, 108
    feelings 6–7
    obligation 49
    opinions 28–29, 108–109
following conversational sequence 66–67, 88–89, 108–109
following directions 15, 16, 18, 19, 35, 38, 56, 78, 98, 101
listening for information 18, 38, 58, 78, 100, 120

Reading Skills
distinguishing True/False statements 9, 30, 50, 59, 70, 73, 92, 101, 112, 121
predicting 79, 121
reading directions 16, 56
reading grammar in context 9, 12, 29, 32, 48, 52, 59, 73, 91, 95, 115
skimming/scanning 10–11, 30–31, 50, 70–71, 92–93, 112–113
reading for information, details 5, 19, 29, 30–31, 34, 39, 44–45, 54, 59, 70–71, 86–87, 92–93, 101, 112–113, 121
relating a story to own experience 17, 57, 99, 102–105

Reading and Writing in the Content Areas

Literature
enjoying literature from around the world 20–23
reading
    a fable 17, 57, 99
    a biography 60–63
    a play 20–23
    an autobiography 102–105
    an interview 14, 34, 54, 74, 96, 116
    classic fiction 39, 40–43, 69, 79, 121
    contemporary fiction 80–85, 122–127
    poetry 37, 77, 119

Science
animal life 18–19, 58–59, 96–97, 100–101, 116–117
dinosaurs 34–35
inventors/inventions 30–31
making a project 16, 56, 98
plants and environment 74–75

Social Studies
agriculture 54
community life 4–5, 24–25, 44–45, 64–65, 86–87, 106–107
environment 74–75
geography 14–15, 54–55, 92–93, 112–113
history 50–51, 55, 60–63
interpreting maps 47
transportation 10–11

Study Skills
taking notes 35, 55, 58, 117
applying logic to solve problems 36, 76, 118
doing research 15, 35, 55, 75, 97, 117
using charts, graphs, and maps 15, 47, 75, 97
preparing oral/written reports 35, 55, 97, 117

Test-Taking Skills
following instructions, taking a variety of test formats 18–19, 38–39, 58–59, 78–79, 100–101, 120–121

Life Skills
asking for/giving directions 46–47
dealing with feelings/health 6–7
getting along in the community 26–27, 46–47, 108–109
ordering food 26–27
talking on the telephone 66–67
shopping 108–109